LAO ZI
THE BOOK OF
THE WAY AND VIRTUE

LAO ZI
THE BOOK OF
THE WAY AND VIRTUE

TRANSLATION AND
COMMENTARY BY
YESHE PALDEN

SEVEN HAWK PUBLISHING

For more information please write:
Seven Hawk Publishing,
326 Wilkes Circle, Santa Cruz, CA 95060.

Printed in the United States by
Ananta Printing and Publishing, Soquel, California.

ISBN 0-9663023-0-3

Dedicated to the memory
of Lama Thubten Yeshe

CONTENTS

ABOUT THE TRANSLATION

The beginning was in Denmark in the late sixties. I came upon Dr. Paul Carus' *The Canon of Reason and Virtue* in a pleasing edition that contained the Chinese text and, as an appendix, a transliteration of each Chinese character. Dr. Carus challenged his readers to make use of this to judge his translation, and, if not satisfied, to make a better one.

What started me off was not dissatisfaction with Paul Carus, but with the existing Danish translations, which represented two extremes: one was scholarly and as dry as old bones, the other a fanciful 'rendering' skimming only the surface. With help of the transliteration, I thought, I can make my own translation word for word, as Lao Zi wrote it.

Foolhardy I started out: "Way can speak of not constant Way." This seemed quite simple, but as I went on an obstacle soon showed up: a passage that didn't make sense. I turned to other translators, but each saw an entirely different meaning. Which one to believe? How far could I trust Paul Carus' transliteration? Sometimes he gave different English words for the same Chinese character, sometimes the same English word for different Chinese characters.

At this critical moment a friend brought me Dr. Wieger's *Chinese Characters* and said: "I don't use this, maybe you can." It was my prayers answered. Now I had the etymology of the Chinese written language and, even better, a dictionary. It didn't take me long before I was able to locate my first character, and lo — it had several more meanings than Paul Carus had given and I could see where some other translator had gotten his ideas; I could begin to evaluate and choose for myself.

Like many at that time I experimented with meditation and hallucinogens. One day I had an experience of profoundly blissful breathing, where "the gates of heaven opened and closed" with every breath. Within a week of this experience a friend showed me a Chinese book on meditation, *The Secret of the Golden Flower,* * and as I leafed through it I came upon a picture of a meditator holding his belly open, and there, in the opening, sat a figure looking out. It struck me as a depiction of the state I had been in, and the next day I bought the book and started to practice the method of concentration that it taught.

At the same time I was working on a word for word translation of Lao Zi, and, as I pondered his words, I noticed how they began to make sense, if I assumed that he was talking about the same teachings as master Lu Zi in *The Secret of the Golden Flower.* Master Lu Zi calls his technique "Circulation of the Light" and says this expression had been revealed by Guan Yin Xi, the disciple that requested the writing of Lao Zi's teachings.† It seemed legitimate to assume a direct lineage from Lao Zi to Lu Zi, and to use the explanations of the latter as a key to a deeper understanding of the former.

I do not mean to say that the common understanding of *The Book of the Way and Virtue* is not valid, but here and there, sometimes concealed, sometimes not, is a second layer of meaning — the esoteric teachings — and all through the text they are the cement that holds together the different exoteric sayings, which so many translators have considered a random collection. I am convinced that the esoteric teachings are the reason that Lao Zi wrote the book; a viewpoint confirmed by the legend that it had been written on request from an adept of Daoist Yoga.

If the esoteric teachings are not understood, then the very heart of the book is neglected; if they are not practiced; then the book is without meaning; because "the Way you can speak of is not the constant Way."

---

* German translation by Richard Wilhelm rendered into English by Gary F. Baines.

† In 1991 Harper San Francisco published a new translation of *The Secret of the Golden Flower* by Thomas Cleary. In this master Lu Zi's technique is called "Turning the light around," and the expression is said to come from Wenshi, also a disciple of Lao Zi.

This viewpoint was radically different from the one held by most translators of that time. They saw breath control as connected with the sometimes naive longevity practices of the popular Daoist religion, which has a bad reputation because of its many superstitious beliefs and sumptuous trappings, far removed from Lao Zi's ideals of simplicity. Even the translators who would admit that Lao Zi was referring to yoga saw it as a digression in a philosophical treatise.

When the translation was finished, I longed to share it with others. I went to a few publishers, but the word was: There is not enough interest on the Danish market to warrant a third translation. I knew of some interest, though, and decided to publish a limited edition myself. I typed stencils (this was before Xerox), printed 200 copies, and bound them Chinese fashion, and this undertaking furnished me with sufficient means to travel to India and Nepal in search of a teacher.

In Nepal I met Lama Thubten Yeshe who became my spiritual friend. He greatly enhanced my understanding of Lao Zi. Buddhist and Daoist teachings are similar in many ways, and Lama Yeshe himself was in all respects an example of the sage as described by Lao Zi: his unselfishness, his simplicity, his humbleness, his ability to help others, his teaching without words. Like Lao Zi, he also knew how to use words to point beyond them; even then, when his English was rudimentary, and this gave me valuable training in understanding the deepest subjects in Pidgin English.

Years later I talked to Lama Yeshe about my beliefs, and I found them difficult to express. Lama Yeshe challenged me by saying that my beliefs were unclear if I could not express them. This book, then, is my belated answer to Lama Yeshe, now in his next incarnation as Lama Ösel.

The Book of the Way and Virtue became my meditation. After I came back from Nepal I found the first edition much too dry and decided to go through it again. It took over a year, but rewarded me with new insights. After I finished it, my life took a turn into a more outwardly active period, and I traveled for several years, ending up in the United States, where I settled down.

Here, in 1984, I crossed again the Daoist path. At the Rainbow Gathering in California a reading of the *Dao De Jing* was advertised. Only three people turned up — "those who know me are few" (70:2). We sat in a solitary part of the forest with a great view over lake and mountains. In our midst we created with sticks and stones the image of *Tai Ji*, the Great Primal Beginning. After a short meditation one person read as long as he/she felt inspired, then sounded a bell and gave the book to the next person.

The translation was by Dr. John C. Wu, and I was pleased with its simple language and the feeling of unity that came through; but something was missing, and again came to me the longing to completely understand what Lao Zi had said. I acquired the book to swiftly make myself a satisfactory English translation, but I did not have my Danish translation or my notes, and soon I was again bogged down in problems. I missed my *Chinese Characters*, but found it at first attempt in a used book store.

This was the year when Lama Yeshe had passed away, and he was brought to life in my mind through the words of Lao Zi. This time I decided to write a commentary, and was thereby forced to express my understanding as Lama Yeshe had urged.

The first English translation was finished late in 1985, and I got a contract with a publisher. What is a contract? Just a piece of paper: The editor who had liked the book left the publisher, and the interest faded. Years passed, but with the possibility of publishing hovering on the horizon I decided to edit the manuscript a final time and to add a word by word transliteration (not included) to go with the commentary and make it unequivocal. This turned out to be as arduous a task as the former three, but thanks to new literature on Daoism and the new translations from the Ma Wang Dui texts, found in China in 1973 in a tomb from the early Han dynasty (206 B.C.- 5 A.D.), I feel that I have come closer than ever to my aim, which is to actualize Lao Zi's teachings now, when the spiritual practices of the East are taking root in the West.

ACKNOWLEDGEMENTS

I want to extend my thanks to Nick Fenger in whose place I sheltered, to Mik Vogelius who gave me *Chinese Characters*, to Hope White for generous help with word processing, to Warren King for a critical first reading, and to Robina Courtin for her enthusiasm that procured some welcome financial help.

Special thanks to Elizabeth Ngo for the gift of a computer and to Marcus Negron for making it work for me.

Obviously I am in debt to many previous translators whose scholarship I have freely put to my use, and whose lucky phrases have often influenced me. For this I give thanks.

Lao Zi - Chinese stone relief

INTRODUCTION

LAO ZI

The author of *The Book of the Way and Virtue (Dao De Jing)* is Lao Zi, the Old Master, who lived in the seventh century B.C. About his life we only know what legend tells us, and nothing in his work connects him with any special place or time. Some people say that he never existed, but we have his book and we have the legend. Must we not believe in legend? The legend is the essence of the human spirit from this far-away time — our own past.

Si Ma Qian (145-86 B.C.) was the first chronicler of China's history. His account of Lao Zi begins with his birthplace and his many names. Born into the family of Li, Plum, which is a symbol of long life, Lao Zi's proper name was Er, Ear. After his death he was called Bo Yang, Prince of the Creative, which is interesting since he always held to the principle of the Receptive, Yin. He was also called Lao Dan, Dan meaning Long Lobes, in Asia a sign of wisdom.

Lao Zi was in charge of the imperial archives in Zhou, and there Confucius came to consult him about the rituals. Si Ma Qian continues his account

Lao Zi said: "Sir, the men of whom you speak are all dead and even their bones have decayed. Only their words exist. Also, Sir, when a noble man finds his time, then he rides a carriage. When he does not find his time he drifts like a winged seed on the wind. I have heard that a good merchant hides his store away as if he had nothing, and a noble man of abundant Virtue acts and looks like a simpleton.

"Sir, let go of your proud airs and many desires, your complacent behavior and excessive ambitions — they will not do you any good! Sir, this is all I have to tell you."

Cunfucius left, and he told his disciples: "I know that birds can fly, that fish can swim, and that beasts can run. Snares can be used for those that run, nets for those that swim, and

15

arrows for those that fly; but the dragon, I do not know how it ascends to heaven on the wind and the clouds. Today I saw Lao Zi; he is like the dragon!"

Lao Zi cultivated the Way and Virtue and his teaching aimed at selflessness and no name. For a long time he lived in Zhou, but when he saw its decline he left. At the pass Yin Xi, the keeper, said to him: "Since you are leaving the world I beg you to write a book for me." Lao Zi therefore wrote a book in two parts explaining the Way and Virtue in some five thousand characters. Then he departed; no one knows whither he went and where he died.

Lao Zi did not find his time. He was a guardian of the Golden Age of the past, but his contemporaries were into other things. So, he drifted away, but the keeper of the pass, true to his call, did not let him go without retaining some of his wisdom.

THE WAY AND VIRTUE

They must have had a lovely time up there in the high pass, the old teacher and the faithful student, while Lao Zi wrote down what the dwellers in the lowlands had not wanted to hear.

How many days did he take? Maybe only a few! It was all clear to him.

Yin Xi already knew about the concepts that Lao Zi would explain: the Way and Virtue. They contain much more than their simple meaning, and todays reader should at least know what Yin Xi knew when he asked for explanation.

Both words refer to the Great Mystery of our being and the universe. The Way is the mystery itself in its absolute aspect; Virtue is the mysterious workings of the Way in the realm of the relative.

Reality seems ever changing, but its true nature remains the same. It is the ultimate ground of everything, the substance of atoms, the extension of space, and the power of forces and fields. Wherever we turn we can see its manifestations; in all phenomena we can search to know what is behind.

Science, as we today understand the term, undertakes an objective study of the outer world, while the mystics subjectively study their own inner world. The Way is the very ground of their being, their feelings, and their thoughts. They ask their questions in this inner sphere, identifying with awareness and observing the physical, mental, and spiritual events. Anyone can do this, and Lao Zi calls it: "Learning no learning and returning to what all men pass by" (64:5), but when the ultimate spiritual event happens, and the knowledge of the Way becomes manifest, it cannot be explained. Only hints can be given.

Science is committed to objectivity, but when it approaches the foundation of all phenomena beyond the realm of the subatomic it discovers the limit of objectivity. Words fail to describe what really is there; only hints can be given, but these hints are often quite similar to those of the mystics, and a dialogue is taking place.*

The true nature of reality cannot be measured or explained, but science recognizes four subtle energies that are instrumental in the formation of the universe: the force of gravity, the electromagnetic force, the strong nuclear force, and the weak nuclear force. So far science only approaches an understanding of their unity in high energy situations such as just after the Big Bang of creation.

Investigating the mystery of life and consciousness the mystics are free to go beyond the measurable and the objective. Still their findings are as 'real' as those of science, and the Daoist practitioners were 'scientific' in their methods and explanations. They see the mystery as threefold: the mystery of awareness, the mystery of breath, and the mystery of reproduction; each linked to a subtle energy. The spirit-energy (shen) causes awareness, the vital breath (qi) animates body and mind, and the vital essence (jing) creates and sustains the continual growth of bodies.

Through these three subtle energies the Way works in the world, and their strength and harmony define the Virtue. At birth the

---

* For example: *The Tao of Physics* by Frithof Capra, Shambala, Berkeley, 1975.

beings have great Virtue, but as we do not know how to conserve the subtle energies they leak away and the Virtue is lost. The actions that conserve Virtue are in themselves virtuous and are defined by unselfishness and simplicity. Virtue can thus be considered dual: outer and inner. The Virtue of action is to comply totally with the Way (21:1), adhering always to the yin principle. The Virtue of being is the sustaining capacity of the Way (51:1-3) by virtue of the subtle energies. In this sense it is a power, but to translate De as 'power' is to neglect the outer aspect. Power can be gathered through yoga, but if it is used for personal profit it has nothing to do with Virtue and leads only to destruction.

Yang and yin originally referred to as sunny and shady

DAOIST YOGA

The writings of Lao Zi are the earliest on Daoism that are preserved, but the teachings they put forth came down through the millennia from the Golden Age.

Chinese history goes back to almost 3000 B.C., when the legendary Fu Xi taught the people trapping and fishing. He was the first emperor of China, and is credited with the invention of the eight trigrams that form the basis for *The Book of Change (Yi Jing)*. After him Shen Nong taught the people agriculture and commerce, and the Yellow Emperor (Huang Di) introduced the weaving of silk and is regarded as the founder of Daoism. Together with Yao and Shun these are the five supreme rulers of the Golden Age that lasted till about 2000 B.C.

It was during this dawn of Chinese civilization that the sages evolved the materials of *The Book of Change* that provides the background and the symbols for both Daoism and Confucianism. It is helpful to shortly consider the ideas in this book, one of the oldest books on earth. It was the aim of the sages to create a method of guidance according to their observations of the changes. They saw these as the cyclic movements of the two primal principles yang and yin, and symbolized them with a whole and a broken line: —— yang is the active, light, creative principle whose image is heaven, – – yin is the passive, dark, receptive principle whose image is earth.

To express the movements the lines were combined one over the other: ⚎ the small yang, ⚌ the big yang, ⚍ the small yin, and ⚏ the big yin. In the cycle of the year, for example, these depict the four seasons: spring, when we go from dark towards light; summer, when the light peaks; autumn, when we go from light towards dark; and winter, when the dark culminates.

By adding another line we get the eight trigrams that Fu Xi according to legend saw in tortoise shells that cracked when heated up. The three lines are read from the bottom up, and they represent earth, man, and heaven. The trigrams are associated with

19

forces in nature: heaven, earth, fire, water, thunder, wind, mountain, and lake, from which their names are derived, but they have many other associations.

The Book of Change in its final form consists of the 64 hexagrams that result from all possible combinations of the eight trigrams. The relation between the two trigrams gives the hexagram its meaning, and each line gets its meaning from its character and placement within the hexagram. Together they form a map of all situations, and king Wen (1150 B.C.) wrote judgements appended to the hexagrams, and his son, the duke of Zhou, to each line, evaluating their potential.

The Book of Change is a guide for right living, but *The Book of the Way and Virtue* is a guide to realization of the primal spirit that is our true nature and ultimate reality.

From the moment of conception, there is in ordinary beings a split between the conscious spirit and the primal spirit. The conscious spirit attaches itself to perceptions, thoughts, and feelings and becomes so entangled with duality that it loses contact with the unity of the primal spirit. The primal spirit is not dead (6:1), but we are unconscious of it. Daoist yoga aims at bringing it into consciousness. As it normally goes in life, we squander our spirit energy because of attachment to desirable objects, just as we dissipate the vital essence through procreation or simply in the pursuit of sexual pleasure. This is how the subtle energies leak away and Virtue is lost.

The method of Daoist yoga is to turn this process around and reverse the flow of the subtle energies. By continence the vital essence is guarded and the vitality of the body is maintained. To turn the conscious spirit from the objects of the senses the adept meditates on breath. When the breath calms down the mind becomes quiet, with time pure awareness illumines the inner world and, in the moment of fulfillment, the primal spirit manifests itself.

THE TEACHINGS

The following is an interpretation of Lao Zi's teachings. The paraphrase of each chapter is preceded by its number.

THE BOOK OF THE WAY

Introduction (Chapters 1-3)

(1) The constant Way evades description; it is the origin of all things. It has a subtle and a gross aspect, and we are caught in the gross by our desires; yet its nature is oneness, and we can experience the wonder of it by giving up desire. (2) In the world all is relative, nothing is absolute. The sage acts spontaneously without selfish motive; he teaches by his example and does not cling to the merit. (3) The sage ruler discourages desire; he enforces what is beneficial; he keeps the ambitious in check, and keeps everything in order by acting without selfish motives.

The Path of Yoga (Chapters 4-10)

(4) If we practice the Way it will not overwhelm us; it will destroy the obstacles and bring harmony and unity, unborn and eternal as it is. (5) There is nothing in heaven or on earth that can save us from the decay and death of all that is manifest, yet the secret is in the breath. We should not waste it in talk, but concentrate on it; (6) thereby we can bring about the stillness that will awaken the primal spirit to consciousness. The work must be continuous but unstrained. (7) In relation to the world, selflessness is our aspiration, and we have nothing to fear by singling ourselves out from the crowd. (8) We should be like water: yielding and humble. In practical matters we should have high ethical standards and, above all, not be contentious. (9) Whether subtle or gross, greed and pride are our downfall. (10) The practice is to be both individual and at one, to soften the breath, and to purify the mind. Then: To rule without cunning, to be always attuned to the spirit, and to make our influence work without enforcement. This is the unselfish power called mysterious Virtue.

Practicing the Path (Chapters 11-16)

(11) The forms are profitable in worldly life, but the practice begins with emptiness; (12) therefore we should choose meditation on breath over the worldly activities, which cannot satisfy, but lead us astray. (13) The ups and downs in the world can only frighten the one who has selfish concerns; without selfishness one comes to terms with the world.

(14) In order to begin the practice in emptiness we sit down and turn our senses toward the formless. Out of confusion comes then guidance toward true knowledge. (15) Those who have gone before us are beyond our comprehension, but we can recognize teachers by certain characteristics, and we should follow their example without thought of success. (16) They have gone beyond life and death. By contemplating death we see how it is necessary to practice and develop while we are alive, because it is in life that we have the opportunity to overcome death.

Practicing in the World (Chapters 17-24)

(17) The master is hardly known in the world; it is other qualities that evoke admiration or contempt. The world does not even know what it owes to the sage. (18) The ways of the world are clothed in pompous language: they are called just and wise, though in reality there is confusion and disharmony. (19) We would do better to abandon the hypocrisy of grand words, and rather cling to the simple virtues and give up superficial knowledge. (20) The emotional discriminations of worldly people lead them to hate and fear each other; their attachment to pleasure makes Lao Zi look weird, but he alone turns to the Way for nourishment. (21) By complying with the Way we gather Virtue. We should not be confused by the images and the things, but only search for the essence, which is real, and therefore confirms our faith. (22) In this way even the perverted becomes perfect, the crooked straight, and the virtues of oneness with the Way develop. (23) We should be wary of words. Only by truly com-

plying with the Way will we gain union with the Way; only by truly gathering Virtue will we gain Virtue. If we court failure, failure will come, (24) and we will achieve qualities opposite to the virtues of oneness with the Way.

The Kings Path (Chapters 25-33)

(25) Lao Zi evokes the nameless chaotic beginning and names it "The Way"; he relates it to the world: heaven, earth, and man. Among men the king is called great, because he follows the Way. (26) His conduct must be dignified and calm, or else all is lost. (27) His acts should be perfect, as well as his concentration, so that he may become a teacher and savior of men and beasts. (28) He should always stick to the yin principle and promote simplicity. (29) His dominion should be derived only from his Virtue, not from interference. (30) He should not use violence, (31) and if he has to, even in victory it should be a cause for regret. (32) He must promote simplicity in the world by his own simplicity; he must know how to stop complications from arising; then he will be like to the life-giving water running in the valley. (33) To obtain this he must have self-knowledge, self-discipline, and perseverance.

Conclusion (Chapters 34-37)

(34) The Way is naturally great without attempting to be so. (35) The Way cannot be taught by talk, it cannot be grasped by the senses, but can only be won by practice. (36) To practice it is to always have the yin attitude. To overcome an opposed force one must actively help it to outgrow itself. Ordinary people will not find enlightenment and should not know the means of government. (37) The king keeps the principles of the Way and the rest comes naturally: Compelled by his unqualified simplicity people will abandon desire, and a Golden Age emerges.

THE BOOK OF VIRTUE
Introduction (Chapters 38-39)

(38) True Virtue transcends the worldly virtues: goodwill, justice, and propriety. Goodwill is acting from the heart, justice is based on cold reasoning, and propriety is mere convention and tries to enforce its preconceived ideas of right and wrong. When the Way and Virtue are lost the human conditions decay. The master does not abandon the solid; (39) he holds on to the one, just as all of nature must do in order to keep its power. If he did not stay at one with the humble he would lose his elevated position.

Virtue of Action (Chapters 40-50)

(40) What makes a person superior is acting in compliance with the Way. Ordinary people laugh at what they cannot see, and they see all true values reversed, as if they had a splinter of the troll's mirror in the eye. The Way cannot be fathomed, but it is our refuge in the beginning as in the end. (41) Turning back and yielding is in accord with the Way. All things were born from it; (42) out of the one came the principles of duality animated by the vital breath, and thus were all things created. According to the balance of yang and yin some are strong and some are weak. The king knows that Virtue's function is weakness, and it is better to belittle oneself than to puff oneself up. All extremes should be avoided. (43) One should teach by example and act without desire. (44) Attachment and greed bring pain; one must know what is enough. (45) One's achievements cannot be seen; what is seen as achievement leads nowhere. The worldly view is upside down, and though everything may seem in some way useful, it is purity and quietness that leads to the goal. (46) When the Way is abandoned the result is war. There is nothing worse than greed. (47) It is not necessary to bustle about to know the truth; the sage stays at home and knows it all. He acts without self-interest. (48) To achieve this, one must discard superficial knowledge; then everything will fall in place. (49)

True Virtue treats all alike; it understands the minds of ordinary people and sees their childish ignorance. (50) People have different aims: Some pursue life, some pursue death, and some sink into the quagmire of materialism. The person of Virtue alone is above the worlds deadly dangers.

The Virtue of Being (Chapters 51-56)

(51) The Way is the source of life, but Virtue is the force that propagates it and brings it to flourish. True Virtue has no self-interest. (52) To gather Virtue we should turn away from the world and follow the Way; we should guard the energies of the vital essence and the spirit and not let them flow out. With a clear and tranquil mind we must turn the light of consciousness around and illuminate the primal spirit. This is to follow the Mother. (53) Following the son takes us far from the Way; (54) following the Mother firmly establishes Virtue in the world. (55) A person of Virtue is like a newborn that as yet has not squandered any life-energy. We should be clear about this and concentrate on the breath in order to still the mind and bring the primal spirit to consciousness; otherwise we grow old and die in vain. (56) Those who know this do not talk about it; they practice it: they guard their life-energy, calm their emotions, and unravel their entanglements; they awaken the primal spirit and are unified with the Way. Thus they are beyond the duality of the emotions.

Ruling with Virtue (Chapters 57-66)

(57) The king's manual begins with a general view of how to rule in peace and in war: too many laws ruin the respect for the law, weapons bring trouble, and education gives rise to cunning and deceit. By not meddling, the ruler brings prosperity to the country. (58) It is not like that in the world today, where the rich acquire their fortune by exploiting the poor, and all values are turned around. It has been like this since the Golden Age. Therefore the king must have strong character, without abusing

the people. (59) It takes an early start if he shall become a leader, comparable to the sage kings of old. (60) It takes great skill to govern; only when the Way prevails can he conquer the demonic forces and enlist their powers on his side. (61) His power is not meant to be used against other countries, but to save and nourish mankind. (62) The Way is the jewel and the refuge. Adversaries can be persuaded, but not by one's alliance with worldly powers; only by holding on to the Way. The Way is the wishfulfilling gem. (63) Act without desire, repay bad with good, and guide the flow of events before they gain momentum. Even the sage does not take affairs lightly. (64) All things start out small, and if they are taken care of they are easily managed. Be as careful in the end as in the beginning. To give up desire and learning, and turn to the Way, is the best means of helping others. (65) Cleverness is a danger, in the people as well as in the ruler. The king must know the difference between cleverness and true insight; that is the supreme Virtue, which leads the people to contentment and docility. (66) The king must be humble in words and action; then everybody will support him. If he does not fight, nobody can fight with him.

Kingly Virtue (Chapters 67-75)

(67) Lao Zi's treasures are compassion, frugality, and humbleness. They allow the king to be brave, generous, and to accomplish the path, so that he can truly lead ordinary people to happiness. The greatest treasure is compassion; even in war it brings victory. (68) Nothing is won by anger and aggression, (69) but rather, if one is attacked, by careful retreat. The one who grieves over the fighting shall win in the end.

(70) Lao Zi's teachings are easy to understand and easy to practice, yet worldly people cannot do so. This is because they do not know the basis of his words. (71) They suffer the sickness of ignorance, and only the one who sees how sick this is can free himself of it.

(72) The king should induce some fear in the people, or they will recklessly go to their ruin. This does not mean that he should weary them in their daily life; neither should he be in awe of his own majesty. (73) It is hard to know when to be daring and when not; both at times can be beneficial. The Way achieves everything without asserting itself, and our actions shall be judged by this standard. (74) The peoples respect for the king is kept alive by the fear of his power over their lives, but if he abuses this power he will injure himself. (75) As it is people are miserable and rebellious because the rulers have no high virtue, but are motivated by pride and greed.

Conclusion (Chapters 76-81)

(76) The yin attitude is superior. (77) Heaven helps the needy; man takes the little they have. Only the man of the Way both has what he needs and cares for the world. (78) The weak overcomes the strong. The king must take upon himself the calamities of the country. (79) If there is conflict, it can never be completely forgotten, therefore one should fulfill one's obligations and not ask anything of others. The Way is always with the good man.

(80) The ideal country is small and peaceful; people are happy to be where they are, and content to live simply. (81) Speak the truth, do not argue, and give up learning. The more one gives to others, the more one has. The Way helps and does not harm.

Further clarification can be found in the commentary that follows the text and is numbered for each chapter and verse.

THE BOOK OF THE WAY

1:1   The Way that you can speak of
is not the constant Way;
the name that you can name
is not the constant name.

-

1:2   Nameless it is the source of heaven and earth;
named it is the Mother of the myriad beings.

-

1:3   Thus always desireless
you may contemplate its wonders;
always having desires
you may contemplate its limits.

-

1:4   These two issue forth together,
but have different names.
Their union is called a mystery,
deepest of mysteries,
door of all wonders.

———

2:1   When all in the world knows beauty to be beauty;
then it is ugly.
When all knows good to be good;
then it is not good.

-

2:2   Because being and non-being gives rise to each other,
difficult and easy complement each other,
long and short compare with each other,
high and low incline toward each other,
song and music harmonize with each other,
before and after follow each other.

-

2:3   Therefore the sage handles his affairs without to-do;
he teaches by deeds, not by words.
He achieves merits, but does not dwell upon them.

Only because he does not dwell upon them
will they not leave him.

_____

3:1   Not exalting the worthy
keeps people from strife;
not prizing goods hard to get
keeps people from theft;
not seeing the desirable
keeps people's hearts undisturbed.
-

3:2   Therefore the rule of the sage
empties their minds,
fills their bellies,
weakens their ambitions,
strengthens their bones.
-

3:3   Always he causes people
to be without calculations and desires,
causes the clever ones to not dare to act.
doing without to-do,
there is nothing that is not in order.

_____

4:1   The Way is vigorous,
but in practice it does not fill you up.
It is deep, oh!
Like the ancestor of the myriad beings.
-

4:2   Blunting the sharp;
untying the tangled;
harmonizing the light;
unifying the dispersed.
-

4:3   So gentle, it seems likely to conserve.
I do not know whose child it could be;
it seems to precede the highest ruler.

_____

5:1   Heaven and earth has no goodwill;

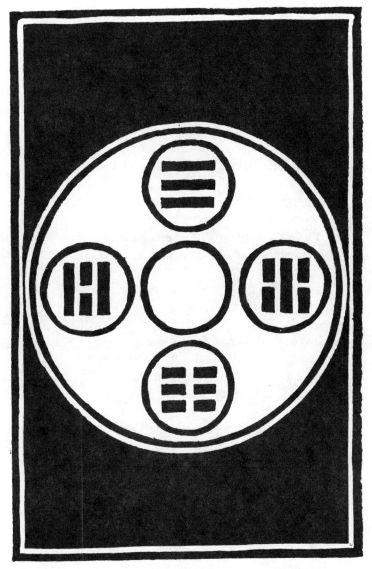

Diagram of the universal power or change.

they treat the myriad beings as strawdogs.
The sage has no goodwill;
he treats ordinary people as strawdogs.
-

5:2 The space between heaven and earth
is like a bellows:
It is empty, yet does not collapse;
it moves, and more comes forth.
-

5:3 Much talk will soon exhaust you;
it is not like observing the center.

_____

6:1 The spirit of the valley does not die;
it is called the mysterious female.
The doorway of the mysterious female
is called the root of heaven and earth.
-

6:2 Continuously, if you will conserve,
practice it without exertion.

_____

7:1 Heaven is lasting, earth is enduring.
Heaven and earth can live long and endure,
because they do not live for themselves.
This is the reason they can live long.
-

7:2 Therefore the sage places himself behind,
yet finds himself ahead;
he places himself outside,
yet finds himself preserved.
-

7:3 Is it not because of his lack of selfish aims
that he can fulfill himself?

_____

8:1 The highest good is like water.
With skill the water benefits the myriad beings
without fighting with them.

It settles in places all men dislike;
therefore it approaches the Way.

-

8:2   For dwelling the ground is good;
in the heart depth is good;
in giving kindness is good;
in speech sincerity is good;
in government rectitude is good;
in affairs efficiency is good;
in action timeliness is good.

-

8:3   Only when not fighting
are you without blame.

———

9:1   To grasp at fullness
is not like stopping.
Testing the keenness,
it cannot long be kept intact.

-

9:2   If the hall is filled with gold and jade
no one will be able to keep it.
If wealth and honor mix with pride
it will certainly lead to disaster.

-

9:3   When the work is done, withdraw.
That is the Way of heaven.

———

10:1   Sustain and guide the animal soul and embrace oneness;
can you be without separation?
Carefully nurse the vital breath, bring about softness;
can you be like a newborn infant?
Wash and clean the mystic mirror;
can you be without blemish?

-

10:2   Love the people and rule the country;
can you be without calculation?

The gates of heaven open and close;
can you act like a female bird?
Clear and pure, penetrating the four directions;
can you do without to-do?

-

10:3   Give life and nourish;
give life, but do not possess;
act, but do not rely upon it;
lead, but do not dominate.
This is called mysterious Virtue.

11:1   Thirty spokes all go to one hub;
the use of the cart comes from the hole.
Take clay to make a vessel;
The use of the vessel comes from the hollow.
Cut out for doors and windows when building a house;
the use of the house comes from the holes.

-

11:2   Thus, by being you can profit,
but you need non-being for use.

12:1   The five colors blind the eye;
the five tones deafen the ear;
the five tastes dull the palate.

-

12:2   Racing and hunting madden the mind;
goods hard to get causes men to do wrong.
Therefore the sage minds the belly, not the eye:
leaving the one he seizes the other.

13:1   Favor and disgrace seem frightening.
Value great afflictions as your own self.

-

13:2   What means: favor and disgrace seems frightening?
Favor conferred upon an inferior
has the effect to frighten.

The loss of it also frightens.
This means favor and disgrace seems frightening.

-

13:3   What means: value great afflictions as your own self?
The reason I have great afflictions
is that I have a self.
When I attain to selflessness
what afflictions can I have?

-

13:4   Thus: he who values the world as himself
can find shelter in the world;
he who loves the world as himself
can be entrusted with the world.

_____

14:1   Looking and not seeing is called: becalm;
listening and not hearing is called: rarefy;
seizing and not getting is called: diminish.
These three cannot be reached by inquiry;
therefore they mix and form one whole.

-

14:2   It is not clear above,
it is not dark below;
unceasing, unnameable,
it returns again to nothing.
It is the form of the formless,
the image of nothing.
It is said to be disturbing and distracting.

-

14:3   Meeting it you will not see its head;
following it you will not see its rear.

-

14:4   When you hold the Way of old
you will have control of the present
and know the ancient beginnings.
This is called: to sort the threads of the Way.

_____

15:1   Those of old who were well versed in the Way
were in touch with hidden wonders and mysteries,
too deep to be fathomed.
Since they cannot be fathomed,
I am forced to describe their appearance:
-

15:2   Careful, as if fording a river in winter;
hesitant, as if fearing their neighbors on all sides;
courteous, they were like the guest;
giving in, like ice about to break up
true, they were like the uncarved wood;
placid, they were like the sea;
steady, as a wind that never stops;
wide open, they were like the valley;
opaque, they were like turbid water.
-

15:3   Who can slowly clear the turbid by quietness?
Who can slowly bring the still to life
by longtime arousing it?
-

15:4   Those who safeguard the Way
do not desire fullness,
because only without fullness
is there no hindrance to new achievements.
———

16:1   Reaching the utmost emptiness;
firmly keeping quiet.
-

16:2   One after another the myriad beings arise,
and thus I contemplate their return.
All mortal beings, all living things,
each goes back and returns to its root.
Returning to the root is called quietness;
it is said to be going back to fate.
Going back to fate is said to be constant;
knowing the constant is called insight.

16:3   If you do not know the constant,
    your errors will make you luckless.
    If you do know the constant you become tolerant;
    being tolerant, you become impartial;
    being impartial, you become kingly;
    being kingly, you become like heaven;
    being like heaven, you become like the Way;
    being like the Way, you become everlasting.
    The body disappears, but there is no danger.

17:1   The existence of the superior man is scarcely known;
    the one a level below him is loved and praised;
    the next one is feared;
    the next again despised.

17:2   When faith is insufficient,
    it does not evoke faith.

17:3   With care he weighs his words;
    he achieves merits and succeeds in affairs
    and everybody says: We just did it naturally.

18:1   When the great Way is abandoned,
    there is goodwill and justice.
    When wisdom and cleverness appear,
    there is great hypocrisy.

18:2   When the six relations are not in harmony,
    there are devoted sons and loving mothers.
    When the country is confused and troubled,
    there are loyal citizens.

19:1   Dismiss holiness, reject cleverness;
    people will profit a hundred times.
    Dismiss goodwill, reject justice;

People will return to being devoted sons
        and loving mothers;
Dismiss cunning, reject profit;
there will be no thieves and robbers.
These three mean that embellishments are not enough.

\-

19:2   Therefore you should depend on this:
look plain and cherish simplicity,
be without selfishness and have few desires,
abolish learning and have no worries.

———

20:1   Agreement and flattery,
how much do they differ?
Like and dislike,
how different do they seem?

\-

20:2   A man who is feared
must likewise fear others.
How unproductive! It has no end.

\-

20:3   Everybody is merry and gay,
as if offering the Grand Sacrifice,
as if ascending a terrace in spring.
I alone have cast anchor;
giving no sign,
like a newborn infant that has not smiled;

\-

20:4   Worn out and exhausted,
like having no place to go;
all men have more than they need;
I alone seem to be left behind.
I am a mindless fool,
so muddled and chaotic.

\-

20:5   Worldly men display such brightness;
I alone am darkly confused.

Worldly men are inquisitive and meddlesome;
I alone am hesitant and reserved.

-

20:6   All men have a purpose;
I alone am thick-headed and vulgar.
I alone am like a stranger among men
and value to be fed by the Mother.

―――

21:1   The demeanor of great Virtue
totally complies with the Way.
When the Way works in beings,
it is both disturbing and distracting.

-

21:2   So distracting, so disturbing,
it contains images.
So disturbing, so distracting,
it contains substance.
So dark, so obscure,
it contains vital essence.
The vital essence is very real;
it contains faith.

-

21:3   From the present back to ancient times,
its name has not left,
thus it saw the beginning of creation.
How do I know about the beginning of creation?
By this!

―――

22:1   Perverted; then perfect.
Crooked; then straight.
Lowly; then filled.
Worn out; then renewed.
Be lacking; then you get.
Have a lot; then you will be deceived.

-

22:2   Therefore the sage embraces oneness,

and is an example for the world.
He does not estimate himself, and so is enlightened;
he is not self-righteous, and so is outstanding;
he does not brag, and so has merit;
he does not pity himself, and so is growing.
Because he does not fight,
nobody in the world can fight with him.
-

22:3   What the ancients said: Perverted; then perfect,
how could that be empty words?
Indeed, perfect and restored.

———

23:1   It is natural to use few words.
Thus a whirlwind does not outlast the dawn;
a torrent does not outlast the day.
Who makes these?
Heaven and earth!
If heaven and earth cannot go on for long,
how much less can man.
-

23:2   Thus engaging in the Way,
you are unified with the Way;
engaging in Virtue,
you are unified with Virtue;
engaging in failure,
you are unified with failure.
-

23:3   Unified with the Way,
the Way is glad to obtain;
unified with Virtue,
Virtue is glad to obtain
unified with failure,
failure is glad to obtain.

———

24:1   On tiptoe you cannot stand;
astride you cannot walk.

24:2   Estimating oneself is not enlightened;
        being self-righteous is not outstanding;
        bragging is without merit;
        self-pity is without growth.

        -

24:3   Those in whom the Way is alive call it:
        gluttony and useless behavior.
        The beings are likely to hate it;
        therefore those who have the Way spurn it.

        ———

25:1   A chaotic thing was already there,
        before heaven and earth came forth:
        so silent, so vast;
        standing alone without change.

        -

25:2   Going everywhere, but not endangering;
        it could thus be the mother of heaven and earth.
        I do not know its name;

        I assign it the character 道 , the Way.

        -

25:3   If forced to describe it, I call it great;
        great I call departing;
        departing I call distant;
        distant I call turning back.

        -

25:4   Thus, the Way is great, heaven is great,
        earth is great, and also the king is great.
        The universe contains four greats,
        and the king is one of them.

        -

25:5   Man follows earth;
        earth follows heaven;
        heaven follows the Way;
        the Way follows its nature.

        ———

26:1   Heavy is the root of the light;
          calm is the master of the quick-tempered.

          -

26:2   This is why the sage during all the day's travel
          does not separate from the heavy baggage-wagon.
          Although there are splendid sights to be seen,
          he stays at ease and lets it all pass by.

          -

26:3   How can he endure,
          the commander of ten thousand chariots,
          if he conducts himself lightly before the world?
          Lightly; then the root is lost.
          Quick-tempered; then the master is lost.

———

27:1   Good walking leaves no track or trace;
          good speech has no flaws or faults;
          good reckoning is done without tablet or tally.

          -

27:2   Good shutting is done without door or fence,
          yet does not open up;
          good fastening is done without tying a cord,
          yet cannot be undone.

          -

27:3   In this way the sage is always good at helping men;
          therefore he does not reject any man.
          He is always good at rescuing beings;
          therefore he does not forget any being.
          This is called: to follow the insight.

          -

27:4   Thus the skillful man
          is the unskillful man's teacher;
          the unskillful man
          is the skillful man's support.

          -

27:5   He who does not revere his teacher,

Heaven, man, and earth.

he who does not love his support,
even if he is clever, is greatly confused.
This is called: working to obtain the wonders.

———

28:1 Knowing his male quality,
adhering to his female,
he is a ravine under heaven.
Being a ravine under heaven,
Virtue will never leave him;
he will again be like a newborn infant.
-

28:2 Knowing his purity,
adhering to his shame,
he is a valley under heaven.
Being a valley under heaven,
he will always have enough Virtue;
he returns again to the uncarved wood.
-

28:3 When the uncarved wood is split,
then there are vessels.
When the sage practices simplicity,
then he becomes the leading official.
Thus the greatest carver does not cut.

———

29:1 If anyone wants to seize the world and interfere,
I do not see how he can succeed.
The world is a spiritual vessel;
it cannot be interfered with.
-

29:2 If you interfere with it,
you will ruin it.
If you grasp it,
you will lose it.
-

29:3 Therefore the sage does not interfere;
thus he ruins nothing.

He does not grasp;
thus he loses nothing.

-

29:4   What others taught I also teach:
a strong and violent man
will not get a natural death.
I will make this my chief instruction.

———

30:1   Those who assist the ruler in accord with the Way,
do not use the force of weapons in the world;
such business tends to pay back.

-

30:2   In places where a legion camped
thistles and thorns will grow.
In the wake of a great army
a year with low yield is certain.

-

30:3   The skillful ones get results and then stop;
they venture not to seize with force.
They get results, but are not conceited;
they get results, but do not brag;
they get results, but are not proud;
they get results, but do not dwell upon it with satisfaction.
This is called: to get results without using force.

———

31:1   Weapons are not auspicious tools;
the beings are likely to hate them.
Therefore, he who has the Way
has no dealings with them.

-

31:2   At home a noble man honors the left;
when using weapons he honors the right.
Weapons are not auspicious tools,
not a noble man's tools.
If he cannot decline the use of them,
indifference to winning is the best.

31:3   Win victory, but do not commend it,
for to commend it is to take pleasure in killing men.
If you take pleasure in killing men,
you will not obtain your worldly ambitions.

-

31:4   In fortunate affairs the left is honored;
in unfortunate affairs the right is honored.
In the army the officers stand to the left;
the commander in chief stands to the right;
that is to say: they deal with it as a funeral ceremony.

-

31:5   When a multitude of men have been killed,
we should weep from grief and sorrow.
Victory in war should be dealt with as a funeral ceremony.

―――

32:1   The Way is forever without name.
Although the uncarved wood is small,
no one in the world is able to subject it.

-

32:2   If kings and princes can keep it,
all beings will spontaneously trust them.
Heaven and earth will unite
and drop sweet dew.
People, without being ordered,
naturally become impartial.

-

32:3   Begin to carve, and you have names.
Once you have names,
you should know how to stop.
If you know how to stop there is no danger.

-

32:4   Compare the Way coming alive under heaven
to a rivulet in a valley,
among the great streams and the sea.

―――

33:1　To know others is cleverness;
　　　to know oneself is insight.
　　　To overcome others require force;
　　　to overcome oneself is strength.
　　　-

33:2　To know satisfaction is wealth;
　　　to act with strength is to be steadfast.
　　　Not to lose one's attainments is to last long;
　　　to die, yet not cease, is longevity.

34:1　The great Way is a flood,
　　　oh, it goes both left and right.
　　　The myriad beings rely upon it for their lives,
　　　and it does not refuse them.
　　　It achieves merits without having a name.
　　　-

34:2　It clothes and feeds the myriad beings,
　　　and does not lord it over them.
　　　Always without desire,
　　　it can be named among the small.
　　　-

34:3　The myriad beings return to it,
　　　yet it does not lord it over them.
　　　It can be named the great.
　　　-

34:4　Because it never makes itself great;
　　　therefore it achieves greatness.

35:1　Grasp the great image;
　　　go out in the world.
　　　going out you will not be hurt;
　　　peace and harmony will prevail.
　　　-

35:2　Where there is music and sweetmeats,
　　　the passing traveller stops.
　　　When the Way is put forth in words,

it is dull and without taste.

-

35:3   Look at it: there is not enough to be seen;
listen to it: there is not enough to be heard;
practise it: there is no end to it.

———

36:1   If you want to restrict something,
you must first expand it;
if you want to weaken something,
you must first strengthen it;
if you want to abandon something,
you must first promote it;
if you want to withdraw something,
 you must first bestow it.
This is called hidden insight:
the soft and weak overcome the hard and strong.

-

36:2   Fish cannot escape from the deep;
therefore the country's sharp tools
should not be revealed to men.

———

37:1   The Way does not do,
yet nothing is not done.
If kings and princes can keep it,
the myriad beings will naturally transform.

-

37:2   Having transformed, if desires arise,
I restrain them with the nameless uncarved wood.
The nameless uncarved wood will bring about no desire.

-

37:3   No desire brings quietness;
the world settles down by itself.

———

THE BOOK OF VIRTUE

38:1 Superior Virtue is not virtuous;
this is why it has Virtue.
Inferior Virtue does not omit virtue;
this is why it has no Virtue.

-

38:2 Superior Virtue is without to-do,
and is not doing for a reason.
Superior goodwill is doing,
but is not doing for a reason.
Superior justice is doing,
and is doing for a reason.
Superior propriety is doing,
and if it is neglected,
it rolls up its sleeve
and casts out the culprit

-

38:3 Thus if the Way is lost there is Virtue;
if Virtue is lost there is goodwill;
if goodwill is lost there is justice;
if justice is lost there is propriety.

-

38:4 Propriety!
Honest faith diluted
and the beginning of trouble.
Beforehand knowledge!
The flower of the Way
and the origin of folly.

-

38:4 Therefore the great man
abides with the solid
and does not dwell on the diluted;
he abides with the fruit
and does not dwell on the flower:
leaving the one he seizes the other.

———

39:1   Of old these attained oneness:
    Heaven attained oneness and became clear;
    earth attained oneness and became calm;
    the spirit attained oneness and became powerful;
    the valley attained oneness and became filled;
    the myriad beings attained oneness and became alive;
    kings and princes attained oneness
    and became pillars under heaven.
    That was the cause.
    -

39:2   Had heaven not thus become clear, it might split;
    had earth not thus become calm, it might erupt;
    had the spirit not thus become powerful, it might cease;
    had the valley not thus become filled, it might be drained;
    had the myriad beings not thus become alive,
           they might be destroyed;
    had kings and princes not thus become
           honorable and noble, they might fall.
    -

39:3   Thus the honorable has its root in the humble;
    the noble has its foundation in the lowly.
    This is why the kings and princes call themselves:
    the orphan, the lonely, and the worthless.
    Does this not show that the humble is their root?
    -

39:4   Thus to cause your honors to be reckoned
    is not honorable.
    Do not wish to be precious like jade,
    but to be left alone like a stone.

40:1   When the superior students hear of the Way
    they diligently act on it.
    When average students hear of the Way,
    they sometimes keep it, sometimes not.
    When inferior students hear of the Way,
    they laugh out loud.

If they did not laugh,
it would not be worthy of being the Way.

\-

40:2   Therefore an established saying has it:
The enlightened Way seems dark;
advance on the Way seems retreat;
the easy Way seems beset with obstacles.

\-

40:3   High Virtue seems low;
great purity seems soiled;
vast Virtue seems lacking;
established Virtue seems false;
plain truth seems faltering.

\-

40:4   The great square has no corners;
the great abilities are achieved late;
the great tone is a rare music;
the great image is without shape.

\-

40:5   The Way is hidden and nameless,
yet only the Way is good at beginning
and good at accomplishing.

———

41:1   Turning back they arouse the Way;
Being weak they practice the Way.

\-

41:2   The myriad things under heaven are born of being;
being is born of non-being.

———

42:1   The Way gave birth to one;
one gave birth to two;
two gave birth to three;
three gave birth to the myriad beings

\-

42:2   The myriad beings carry yin on their back
and yang in their bosom,

harmonized by the vigor of vital breath.

42:3   Hence beings either lead or follow,
either are warmhearted or puffed up,
either are strong or frail,
either sustain or destroy.

42:4   What men hate is to be orphan, lonely, or worthless;
yet kings publicly style themselves thus.
Therefore beings either diminish and benefit by it,
or they increase and are harmed.

42:5   Because of this the sage puts an end to excess,
puts an end to extravagance,
puts an end to extremes.

43:1   The softest thing under heaven
overruns the most solid.
Non-being enters no-crack;
hence I know the benefit of not-doing.

43:2   Teaching without words
and the benefit of not-doing
are rarely attained under heaven.

44:1   Your name or your body, which is dearest?
Your body or your possessions, which are worth most?
Gain or loss, which is most sickening?

44:2   Because too much love
will certainly bring great spending;
abundant hoarding
will surely entail great loss.

44:3   Know when you have enough, and there is no disgrace;
know when to stop, and there is no danger;

thus you can grow old.

———

45:1   Great achievement seems defective;
its practice is not harmful.
Great fullness seems vigorous;
its practice will exhaust you.

-

45:2   Great honesty seems crooked;
great skill seems clumsy;
great eloquence seems stammering.

-

45:3   Restlessness overcomes cold;
quietness overcomes heat
Purity and quietness are first in the world.

———

46:1   When the world has the Way,
riding horses are left to drop manure;
when the world is without the Way,
war horses are bred in the suburbs.

-

46:2   There is no greater crime than many desires;
there is no greater misfortune
          than not knowing what is enough;
there is no greater fault than the wish to acquire.
Therefore one who knows that enough is enough
always has enough.

———

47:1   Without going out the door,
you can know the world;
without looking out the window,
you can see the Way of heaven.

-

47:2   The farther you go,
the less you know.

-

47:3   Therefore the sage knows without going about;
he names without seeing;
he achieves without doing.

————

48:1   Pursuing learning every day one accumulates;
pursuing the Way every day one loses;
one loses and loses again,
in order to attain to not-doing.
Nothing doing, yet nothing is not done.
-

48:2   To win the world,
always be without involvement.
To grasp it with involvement
is not enough to win it.

————

49:1   The sage has no fixed mind;
thus everybody's mind is his mind.
-

49:2   Towards the good I am good;
towards the bad I am also good.
Virtue is good.
towards the faithful I am faithful;
towards the unfaithful I am also faithful.
Virtue is faithful.
-

49:3   The sage is alive in the world,
amiable and compliant;
his heart encompasses the world.
Ordinary people lend him their ears and eyes;
to the sage they are all children.

————

50:1   Between birth and death,
three in ten follow life,
three in ten follow death,
men whose lives move into dead ground
are also three in ten.

Why is that?
Because they live in the thick of life.

-

50:2   Indeed, I heard that those
who are good at preserving life
can travel overland without meeting yak or tiger,
can enter the army without suffering armor or weapon.
The yak finds no spot to butt its horn;
the tiger finds no place to put its claws;
the weapon finds no spot to lodge its blade.
Why is that?
Because there is no ground for death in them.

51:1   The Way gives them life;
Virtue nourishes them;
substance shapes them;
influence completes them.

-

51:2   Therefore all beings without exception
venerates the Way and values Virtue.
That the Way is venerated and Virtue valued,
is not by any command,
but always spontaneous.

-

51:3   Thus the Way gives them life,
and Virtue nourishes them,
makes them grow and rears them,
balances them and directs them,
supports them and protects them
This is how the myriad beings arise
and do not refuse life and nourishment.

-

51:4   To give life, but not possess;
to act, but not rely upon it;
to lead, but not dominate.
This is called supreme Virtue.

52:1   The world has a source,
which is the Mother of the world.
When you get hold of the Mother,
you will know the son;
when you know the son,
turn back and keep to the Mother.
The body disappears, but there is no danger.

-

52:2   Seal the pleasure-gate, shut the doors;
your whole life there is no toil.
Open the pleasure-gate, have numerous involvements;
your whole life is beyond rescue.

-

52:3   To see the small is called insight;
to keep to the yielding is called strength.

-

52:4   Use the light:
turn it back and restore your insight,
without leaving anything to harm yourself.
This is called: to practice the constant.

———

53:1   Applying the bit of knowledge I have,
I walk along the great Way;
to stray is my only fear.
The great Way is very easy,
but people love shortcuts.

-

53:2   The court is very clean;
the fields are grown over with weeds;
the granaries are completely empty.

-

53:3   Some wear stylish clothes in many colors,
and girdle themselves with sharp swords;
they eat and drink till satiation,
and have an excess of valuable goods.
This is called vanity of robbers;

The mandala of the Golden Flower

it is far from the Way.

———

54:1   What is well established is not uprooted;
what is firmly held does not slip away.
Thus it will be worshipped for generations without end.

-

54:2   Cultivated in yourself,
Virtue will be genuine;
cultivated in your family,
Virtue will be ample;
cultivated in your neighborhood,
Virtue will be growing;
cultivated in your country,
Virtue will be abundant;
cultivated in the world,
Virtue will be universal.

-

54:3   Therefore consider yourself as a person;
consider your family as a family;
consider your neighborhood as a neighborhood;
consider your country as a country;
consider the world as a world.
How do I know that the world is so?
By this!

———

55:1   He who is generously endowed with Virtue
is like a naked infant;
wasp and scorpion do not sting him,
venomous snakes do not bite him,
savage tigers do not maul him,
birds of prey do not seize him.

-

55:2   His bones are weak, his sinews soft,
yet his grip is firm;
he knows not of the union of male and female,
yet his penis rises;

his vital essence is perfect.
He can cry all day without getting hoarse;
his harmony is perfect.

-

55:3   Knowing harmony is called constant;
knowing the constant is called insight.
Increasing life is called auspicious;
applying the mind to the vital breath
is called strength.

-

55:4   When beings are healthy,
and then become decrepit,
it is called: not the Way.
What is not the Way soon ends.

_____

56:1   One who knows does not speak;
one who speaks does not know.

-

56:2   Seal the pleasure-gate
shut the doors;
blunt the sharp;
untie the tangled;
harmonize the light;
unify the dispersed.
This is called primordial union.

-

56:3   Thus you can neither be intimate nor distant,
you can neither be helped nor hurt,
you can neither be honored nor despised.
For this the world will honor you.

_____

57:1   Use straight means to rule the country;
use extraordinary means to wage a war;
be without involvement to win the world.
How do I know it is like that?
By this!

57:2　When there are many taboos in the world,
　　　people are very poor;
　　　when people have many sharp tools,
　　　there is growing confusion in the country;
　　　when men are very clever and cunning,
　　　abnormal things begin to multiply;
　　　when many rules and regulations are announced,
　　　there are more thieves and robbers.
　　　-

57:3　Therefore the sage says:
　　　I am without to-do,
　　　and people by themselves transform;
　　　I appreciate quietness,
　　　and people spontaneously straighten out;
　　　I am without involvement,
　　　and people by themselves become wealthy;
　　　I have no desires,
　　　and people naturally become like uncarved wood.

58:1　When government is hesitant and reserved,
　　　people are pure and sincere;
　　　when government is inquisitive and meddlesome,
　　　people are broken and needy.
　　　-

58:2　Oh! Misfortune is what luck is leaning on;
　　　oh! Luck is what misfortune is prostrating to.
　　　Who knows how far it will go?
　　　It is not straightforward.
　　　-

58:3　The straightforward has turned abnormal,
　　　the good has become strange;
　　　thus men have been spellbound
　　　since the days of old.
　　　-

58:4　Therefore the sage

is square, but not cutting;
is angular, but not hurting;
is straight, but not reckless;
is bright, but not blinding.

———

59:1   In ruling men and serving heaven,
there is nothing like saving up,
but saving up means early submission.
Early submission brings a heavy store of Virtue.

-

59:2   With a heavy store of Virtue,
there is nothing you cannot subdue;
when there is nothing you cannot subdue,
no one knows your limits.

-

59:3   When no one knows your limits;
then you can have the country.
When you have the country's Mother;
then you can grow old.
This is called: deep roots and firm foundation,
the Way of long life and ancient vision.

———

60:1   Ruling a great country
is like cooking small fish.

-

60:2   When the Way is present under heaven,
the demons have no power.
Not that the demons are without power,
but their power does not harm men.

-

60:3   Not only does their power not harm men,
but the sage also does not harm them.
The two does not harm each other;
therefore their Virtues blend and come together.

———

61:1   A great country is downstream;

65

it is the confluence of the world;
it is the female of the world.
By quietness the female always overcome the male;
in order to be quiet she keeps low.

-

61:2 Hence, if a great country
keeps lower than a small country,
it will conquer the small country.
If a small country keeps lower than a great country,
it will conquer the great country.
Therefore you either take the lower position,
      and thus conquer;
or you have the lower position and conquer.

-

61:3 All a great country wants
is to include and feed more men;
all a small country wants
is to enter the service of mankind.
They can both get what they want,
but the great must take the lower position.

62:1 The Way is hidden in the myriad beings;
the good man's jewel,
the bad man's refuge.

-

62:2 Fair words can be used in the market;
noble deeds can add to a man.
If a man is not good,
how can he be rejected?

-

62:3 Therefore, when the emperor is crowned,
and three ministers are installed,
although you might be there,
bending and holding the jade disc,
preceded by teams of horses,
it is not like sitting down advancing in the Way.

62:4   There is a reason why the ancients valued the Way.
        Did they not say: It gives what you ask for;
        it forgives your wrongdoings?
        Therefore the world values the Way.

        ─────

63:1   Do without to-do;
        serve without involvement;
        taste the tasteless.

        -

63:2   Great or small, many or few,
        repay injuries with Virtue.

        -

63:3   Plan the difficult while it is easy;
        tackle the great while it is trifling.

        -

63:4   The difficult affairs under heaven
        certainly arose from the easy;
        the great affairs under heaven
        certainly arose from the trifling.
        Therefore the sage never does anything great;
        thus he is able to achieve greatness.

        -

63:5   Those who lightly assent
        are seldom trustworthy;
        those who think much is easy
        will surely find much difficult.
        Therefore the sage treats things as difficult;
        thus he is always without difficulties.

        ─────

64:1   What is at rest is easy to maintain;
        what has no symptoms is easy to plan;
        what is brittle is easy to break;
        what is small is easy to scatter.

        -

64:2   Act on it before it is there;
        direct it before trouble arises.

64:3   A tree that matches a man's embrace
grows from a downy sprout;
a nine-tiered terrace
rises from a hodfull of earth;
a journey of a thousand miles
begins under your feet.

-

64:4   When people pursue an affair,
it is always at the verge of success that they ruin it.
Be as careful in the end as in the beginning;
then no affairs will be ruined.

-

64:5   Therefore the sage desires no desire;
he does not value goods hard to get.
He learns no learning,
and returns to what all men pass by.
Thus he helps the myriad beings in their nature,
but he dares not to act.

———

65:1   Those of old who were well versed in the Way
did not try to enlighten the people;
they would rather see to it that they were simple.
People are difficult to rule
when they are too clever.

-

65:2   Thus to use cleverness to rule a country
is to ruin the country.
Not to use cleverness to rule a country
is to bless the country.

-

65:3   Those who understand these two
have a pattern to follow.
Always knowing the pattern to follow
is called supreme Virtue.

65:4 Supreme Virtue is deep;
   it is distant;
   it helps the beings turn back.
   Afterwards there is complete compliance.

   ———

66:1 The great streams and the sea
   can be king of all the valleys,
   because they excel in keeping low.
   Thus they can be king of all the valleys.

   -

66:2 Therefore, if you want to be above the people,
   your words must place you below them;
   If you want to be ahead of the people,
   you must place yourself behind them.

   -

66:3 Thus the sage stays above,
   but the people are not oppressed;
   he stays ahead,
   but the people are not hurt.

   -

66:4 Therefore the world is pleased to push him forward,
   and does not weary of him.
   Since he does not fight,
   nobody can fight with him.

   ————

67:1 All in the world say that my Way is great,
   it is like nothing else.
   Because of its greatness
   it is like nothing else;
   if it was like anything else,
   it would soon have been tiny.

   -

67:2 I have three treasures,
   which I keep and protect.
   The first is compassion,

the second is frugality,
the third is not daring
to be ahead in the world.
-

67:3   Being compassionate,
you can be brave;
being frugal,
you can be generous;
not daring to be ahead in the world,
you can attain the abilities to lead.
-

67:4   Nowadays they do without compassion,
and will also be brave;
they do without frugality,
and will also be generous;
they do without humbleness,
and will also be ahead.
That is death!
-

67:5   Thus compassion brings victory in war
and gives firmness in defense.
When heaven wants to help someone,
it guards him with compassion.

———

68:1   Good officers are not fierce;
good fighters are not furious.
Those who are good at defeating the enemy,
do not engage with him;
those who are good at using men
put themselves under them.
-

68:2   This is called: the Virtue of not fighting;
this is called: to use the strength of men;
this is called: to match the highest heaven of old.

———

69:1   Commanders of armies have a saying:

I dare not play the master,
but play the guest;
I dare not advance an inch,
but retreat a foot.

-

69:2　This is called: to advance without advancing,
to roll up the sleeve without baring the arm,
to throw without the opponent,
to hold without weapons.

-

69:3　There is no greater misfortune
than taking the enemy lightly;
by taking the enemy lightly
I risk to lose my treasures.

-

69:4　Thus, when opposing armies meet,
the one who feel sorrow shall conquer.

―――

70:1　My words are very easy to understand,
very easy to act on.
In the world no one can understand them,
no one can act on them.

-

70:2　My words have ancestors,
my deeds have a ruler.
It is because these are not known,
that I am not known.
Those who know me are few,
but by them I am valued.

-

70:3　Thus the sage wears coarse wool
and conceals the jade in his bosom.

―――

71:1　To know the not known is superior;
not to know the known is sickness.
Only if you are sick of sickness,

will you not be sick.

-

71:2 The sage is not sick,
because he is sick of sickness;
therefore he is not sick.

The intermingling of yin and yang.

72:1 If people do not fear your might,
then something more mighty will come.

-

72:2 Do not intrude in their homes;
do not overburden them with work.
Only if not wearied,

will they not weary of you.

-

72:3   Thus the sage knows himself,
but does not estimate himself;
he loves himself,
but does not prize himself.
Thus leaving the one he seizes the other.

―――

73:1   The courage to dare causes killing;
the courage to not dare brings life.
These both can either benefit or harm;
what heaven hates, who knows the reason?
Therefore the sage considers it difficult.

-

73:2   The Way of heaven does not fight,
yet is good at overcoming;
it does not speak,
yet is good at responding;
it is not summoned,
yet comes by itself;
it rests tranquil,
yet is good at planning.

73:3   Heavens net is vast and wide;
though coarse, it loses nothing.

―――

74:1   If people do not fear death,
they cannot be made to tremble by death.
If people are kept in constant fear of death,
and want to do something extraordinary,
when I can apprehend them and kill them, who dares?

-

74:2   There is always the Reaper who does the killing.
To take the place of the Reaper and do the killing
is called to take the place
        of the master carpenter and chop.

Those who take the place
            of the master carpenter and chop,
rarely escape wounding their hands.

———

75:1   People starve because their superiors
            eat up too much in taxes;
therefore they starve.
People are hard to rule because their superiors
            are too active;
therefore they are hard to rule.
People take death lightly because they aim
            at the gifts of life;
therefore they take death lightly.
-

75:2   Those who have no use for life
are worthier than those who prize life.

———

76:1   When a man is born he is soft and weak;
when he is dead he is hard and stiff.
When plants and trees come forth
they are soft and tender;
when they have died they are withered and dry.
-

76:2   Thus hard and stiff are companions of death;
soft and weak are companions of life.
Because of this a strong army will not win;
a strong tree will break.
-

76:3   Strong and great stay below;
soft and weak stay above.

———

77:1   The Way of heaven is like a bow that is drawn:
the high is curbed, the low is raised up.
Those who have too much are taken from;
those who have not enough are given to.
-

77:2   The Way of heaven takes from those who have too much

and gives to the ones who have not enough.
The way of men is not like this:
they take from those who have not enough
in order to attend to those who have too much.

-

77:3   Who is able to have more than enough,
and also attend to the world?
Only those who have the Way.

-

77:4   Thus the sage acts, but he does not rely upon it;
he achieves merits, but does not dwell upon them;
he does not want his worth to be apparent.

———

78:1   Nothing in the world
is more soft and weak than water,
yet in attacking the hard and strong
nothing surpasses it;
nothing can take its place.

-

78:2   The weak overcomes the strong;
the yielding overcomes the hard.
No one in the world does not know,
but no one is able to act on it.

-

78:3   Therefore the sage says:
He who accepts the dirt of the country,
is said to be master of the fertility shrine.
He who accepts the misfortunes of the country,
is king of the world.
Straight words seem paradoxical.

———

79:1   To reconcile great enmity
is sure to leave some enmity.
How can this be good?

-

79:2   Therefore the sage takes the debtors part of the contract

and does not require anything from others.
Those who have Virtue care for a contract;
those who have no Virtue try to suppress it.
-

79:3　The Way of heaven favors no one,
but is always with the good man.

———

80:1　A small country with few people.
Let them have several men with abilities of a chief,
but not use them.
Let them take death seriously,
and not move to distant places.
-

80:2　Although they have boats and carriages,
there are no places to go to;
although they have armors and weapons,
there are no occasions to display them.
-

80:3　Let men return to knotted cords,
and use them.
Their food is delicious,
their clothes beautiful;
their homes are peaceful,
their customs pleasing.
-

80:4　The neighboring country can be seen in the distance,
they can hear the sounds of dogs and roosters,
but the peoples reach old age and die
without having dealings with each other.

———

81:1　Truthful words are nor fair;
fair words are not truthful.
The good do not argue;
those who argue are not good.
Those who know have no wide learning;
those with wide learning do not know.

81:2 The sage does not hoard;
the more he does for others,
the more he has;
the more he gives to others,
the greater his bounty.

-

81:3 The Way of heaven is to help and not harm;
the Way of the sage is to act without strife.

Simplicity.

COMMENTARY

1:1

Dao, the Way, is Lao Zi's name for the ultimate reality behind all relative phenomena. In the opening verse he describes its essence: forever unchanging, it transcends all explanations. We are thus warned that the words can only point towards the Way like a finger points at the moon, and we should not be like the dog who looks at the finger without realizing its purport.

There are many names: Allah, Brahman, Dao, God, Isis, Jehova, Nagual, Oludumare, Shunyata, Wakan Tanka, but none is the eternal name, which is beyond our grasp.

1:2

The second verse describes the images of the Way.

The nameless ultimate reality is the source of the universe. The universe is dual in nature, polarized in the two primal forces: yang and yin, whose images are Heaven and Earth.

From the earliest times in China the nameless source was worshipped in the image of the Mother, giving life to all beings.

1:3

The third verse is about the substance of the Way.

Our desires determine how we may observe the Way. Only if we rid ourselves of our craving for life can we penetrate to the spiritual essence of the Way; as long as we are beset by desires we are bound to the material.

In this Lao Zi is in agreement with other great religions. Mahatma Gandhi summarized the central scripture of Hinduism, *Bhagavad-Gita*, in one word: Desirelessness; and of the Buddha's four noble truths the two central ones hold that the cause of suffering is the craving for life, and that the cessation of suffering comes with the cessation of this craving.

1:4

The spiritual and the material are not two different things, they are two aspects of the Way. Even without desires we are still living in the world, and it is only by unifying the spiritual and the material that we can enter through "the door of all wonders" (see commentary 6:1). We should be able to say with Christ: "I am in the world, but not of the world."

2:1

The world, literally: under heaven, always means the worldly and ordinary as opposed to the noble and true.

In the world of phenomena nothing is constant, nothing is absolute. There is no absolute beauty, no absolute good, and the dogmatic assertion that there is, turns beautiful into ugly and good into evil, as we see when fundamentalists take the written word to be absolute truth.

2:2

In the world all is relative.

That the manifest and the unmanifest give rise to each other is illustrated in subatomic research by certain processes that can only be understood if one supposes particles to come into existence out of nothing and, after a fraction of a second, to disappear again.

2:3

The sage handles his affairs without to-do. This refers to the ideal way of acting without desire. When we have no ulterior motives we permit the Way to act through us: as we perceive the need for a certain action we spontaneously perform it without thinking of the advantage or disadvantage it may have for ourselves. This is the opposite of acting upon desire. When there is desire, there is a calculation of how to satisfy the desire, and there is a corresponding disregard for the influence it may have on others.

Selfless action will bring benefit and merit to ourselves, though this was not what motivated us, but if we dwell on the merit we are caught in pride, and the merit is lost. Tibetan Buddhists dedicate their merit to the benefit of all sentient beings; that has the same meaning.

3:1

This verse shows how Lao Zi's path of no-desire is the complete opposite of the ways of our times. But one should not think that being without desire precludes enjoyment. When Lao Zi describes the ideal state, he says about people: "Their food is delicious, their clothes beautiful; their homes are peaceful, their customs pleasing." (80:4)

3:2

An empty mind is the condition for the practice of the Way. The belly is considered to be the seat of life and should be filled with vital breath. Ambitions are just obstacles on the Way, and strengthening the bones refers according to Qi Bo, the teacher of the Yellow Emperor, to the cultivation of the vital essence, that causes the bones to be filled with marrow.

3:3

Knowledge engenders desire, and desire leads to selfish action. Such actions based on pride, greed, or fear have no consideration for the whole and therefore bring disorder. The sage ruler prevents this by his own example. In *Bhagavad-Gita* it is said: "What a great man does, ordinary people will imitate; they follow his example."*

Doing without to-do, as explained in commentary 2:3, does only what is needed; therefore everything will be in order.

4:1

The first two lines have been translated in many different ways.

---

* The Song of God: Bhagavad-Gita translated by Swami Prabhavananda and Christopher Isherwood. The American Library, New York, p. 47

Most translators read *zhong*, an empty bowl, for *chong*, rush, dash, or vigorous, and we have: "The Way is empty, yet in use it is never filled up." or: "The Way is empty, yet when used it never needs to be filled up." Some also read *qing*, exhausted, for *ying*, filled up, and we have: "The Way is empty, yet in use it is never exhausted."

I think *chong* refers to the creative power of the Way, and how can the Way be used except by practicing it? The creative power of the Way may seem overwhelming, but instead of filling us up it will help us empty our minds of opinions and desires, if we live according to its principles and practice it in order to realize it.

4:2

The Way is doing away with extremes because of the cyclic character of all phenomena. When yang peaks yin begins to rise and vice versa. (See also commentary 56:2)

5:1

Strawdogs were made for offering, thus they were first blessed, then thrown on the trash heap. This is like our situation in the world: however exalted we are in life, it is certain that we shall die. Even the sage cannot save us. This is the reason why we must practice now, since we never know when death will come.

5:2

According to *The Book of Change*, what comes out of the space between heaven and earth is the fate of men; but there is a hidden meaning in this verse. In the eighth wing of *The Book of Change*, Discussion of the Trigrams, it is said: "The Creative manifests itself in the head, The Receptive in the belly."* Thus the bellows between heaven and earth are the lungs, and what comes out is the breath, and with it consciousness.

---

* I Ching the Richard Wilhelm translation rendered into English by Gary F. Baines. Princeton University Press, Princeton, July 1967, p. 247.

5:3

If we use our breath to talk we exhaust the energies of the body. Instead we should use the breath to gather vital energy and thereby reverse the flow of energy. This is the way to overcome death. When the primal spirit is awakened into consciousness, as the next chapter describes, it will survive the death of the body. (16:3, 33:2, 52:1)

6:1

This verse is found in Lie Zi as a quote from *The Book of the Yellow Emperor*, and it contains ancient symbolic images pertinent to Daoist yoga.

"The spirit of the valley" is the primal spirit. The valley stands for openness. When you call into the valley, it will fill with sound and this is called the spirit of the valley and is a symbol of the primal spirit. It can never die since it is the active creative force of the Way, but in the beings, from the moment of conception, it is separated from the conscious spirit and dwells in unconsciousness until death. In the trigram ☵ *Kan*, Water, the spirit is symbolized by the one yang line while the two yin lines symbolizes the receptive valley.

"The mysterious female" is another name for the same thing. The two yin lines then symbolizes the womb of unconsciousness, the yang line the primal spirit as a fetus. "Female" means quietness (61:2), and "mysterious" refers to the spirit being alive in the quietness (15:3).

"The doorway of the mysterious female" is the same as "the door of all wonders" (1:4). Through this door the primal spirit is born into consciousness. To make this happen the conscious spirit must be turned back and directed inwards in meditation instead of dissipating its energy in pursuit of the objects of the senses, as it normally does.

The conscious spirit is symbolized by the trigram ☲ *Li*, Fire. Outside is the clarity of awareness, but inside the darkness of worldly duality is ruling. The awakening of the primal spirit into consciousness is known as "taking from *Kan* to fill in *Li* "; the one yang line in Water is transferred to Fire to constitute the trigram of the enlightened spirit ☰ *Qian,* Heaven, and the one yin line from Fire is thereby transferred to Water to constitute the trigram ☷ *Kun,* Earth. This is why the door is called the root of heaven and earth.

This door has no physical existence but is the image of a point of transition between being and non-being. It is the same as the door of creation, and also in that sense is it the root of heaven and earth. To go back through the door of creation and merge with the Mother of all beings is the goal of Daoist yoga, and it is connected with the interaction of spirit and water just as the creation in Genesis 1:1-2: "In the beginning God created heaven and earth...And the spirit of God moved upon the face of the waters."

6:2

In order to conserve the energy of the vital breath the breathing must be like that of a newborn infant (10:1). It is a subtle practice, a watchful letting go, rather than using exertion.

7:1

The Daoists emphasize the importance of a long life because it takes time to revive the spirit. Lao Zi says: "The great abilities are achieved late." (40:4).

7:2

If one has to fall back in the race for worldly success and stay outside the mainstream in order to practice, one has nothing to fear; the Way gives protection (50:2, 55:1).

Shri Krishna said: "If a man will worship me...I shall supply all his needs, and protect his possessions from loss."* In the end one comes out ahead because, when death comes, only the inner qualities count.

---

* *Bhagavad-Gita,* p 83.

7:3

The paradox is that unselfish actions really benefits the self, while selfish actions hurt the self.

8:1

Water is the great symbol of the Way, not repelled even by settling in the gutter. The way of water is dear to Lao Zi, serving as a model for the yogi. When he talks of the Way in terms of yin, it is not that the Way is more yin than yang, but that we, if we want to approach the Way, must give up our individual self-will and adopt the yin attitude of compliance (21:1, 65:4).

8:2-3

Although there is no absolute good to be found in the world, there are things that are beneficial for the practitioner.

9:1

To be filled up with desires, emotions, knowledge, and opinions is not the Daoist goal, and even the keenness of a mind in practice is to be left alone, lest in testing it, it may be lost.

9:2

The way of greed and pride is in contrast to the way of water. Here, as often, Lao Zi is close to Jesus who said: "Lay not up for yourselves treasures upon earth, where moth and rust doth corrupt, and where thieves break through and steal." (Matt. 6:19).

9:3

These were not empty words; after this book was written Lao Zi withdrew and it was the last ever heard from him.

10:1

This chapter is essential in exposing the path of yoga. A key to its understanding is the hexagram ䷊ *Tai*, Peace, that pictures the union of heaven and earth and is a specially favorable hexagram.

The three questions in this verse correspond to the three active yang lines of the lower trigram and is concerned with the inner aspect of the practice, and with that which comes before the completion.

The first question mentions the animal soul, *po*, meaning the part of our psyche that is occupied with the needs and wants of the body. This has to be sustained and guided, since we do live in the material world, but at the same time we must embrace the great oneness, in which our body is a tiny part. Can we unify these two aspects without a split?

The second question corresponds to one of the ruling lines in the hexagram. It talks of breath meditation, asking if we can let the breath be as natural as that of a newborn infant, since the practice of breathing is without exertion (6:2).

The third question is whether we can purify the inner mirror by cleaning out all selfish calculations and desires that hinder the clear reflection of the Way in our minds.

10:2

The three questions in this verse correspond to the three passive yin lines of the upper trigram of the hexagram *Tai*, Peace, and are concerned with the outer aspects of the yogic achievements. There is a correspondence line by line with the lower trigram.

The first line is again about the relations to the world of substance: can you govern the country without imposing your will?

The second question again corresponds to a ruling line. This time the image is a female bird and it is explained thus: When a hen is hatching her eggs they are constantly in her mind and at any moment she responds to the call of the spirit. The opening of the gates signifies the Creative, the closing signifies the Receptive.* Can you be active and passive with complete responsiveness to the prompting of the spirit?

The last question refers to the final achievement of the essence

---

* See *I Ching*, p 318.

of the Way. The purification is fulfilled, the mystic mirror is without blemish and clearly reflects all things near and far. Now, can you do without to-do?

10:3

Being creative, active, and a leader, without any selfish motive, that is mysterious Virtue.

11:1-2

In this chapter Lao Zi shows how emptiness is useful. Out of being we can make profit, but when it comes to using the Way, i.e: practicing it, then the mind must be empty (3:2).

12:1

The five colors are: red, yellow, green or blue, white, and black. The five tones are: c, d, e, g, and a. The five flavors are: salty, bitter, sour, biting (hot), and sweet.

12:2

The belly is the seat of life, the gathering place of vital breath, while the eyes here stand for the senses and their outward turned activities.

13:1-2

The ups and downs in life are frightening; even when heaven shows favor it is frightening, because eventually we will be treated like strawdogs (5:1).

13:3

We only fear life's afflictions because we are attached to ourselves. The bodhisattva, the enlightened being who lives only to help others, is fearless.

14:1

He Shang Gong entitled this chapter "Clearing up the mystery". It is an important chapter on yoga, giving instructions in sitting practice.

"Looking and not seeing" describes a way of keeping the eyes passive, neither looking outward nor looking within, just sensing brightness without looking. This use of the eyes has the effect to make one feel at ease, firm, calm, and unified. The word *yi*, becalm, has all this meanings.

"Listening and not hearing" means to listen to the absolutely silent flow of breath through the nose. This rarefies the breath, both in the sense of refining it, and in the sense of actually less air passing.

The breath is allowed to be totally free and one watches it as concentrated as a cat watching a mouse hole. This is the meaning of "seizing and not getting", and it diminishes the mind's content of knowledge and desire, so that the conscious spirit in time can become aware of the primal spirit.

These instructions must be put into practice to be understood, they can not be grasped intellectually.

14:2

In the beginning of sitting meditation there is nothing to hold on to and one can expect a certain amount of confusion. The two obstacles to concentration are the disturbance of agitated mind and the distraction of dullness.

14:3

If we persevere, we will find what we seek and be able to follow it without ever seeing its beginning or its end.

14:4

When finally union with the Way is achieved it brings miraculous powers; by this all is known.

15:1-3

This chapter describes those who have sorted the threads of the Way.

Who can do what these old yogis did: find clarity in the quietness of meditation and bring the primal spirit to life? (6:1)

15:4

The last line gives difficulties. *Pi*, conceal, darken, or hinder talents in developing, is by most translators read as *pi*, worn out, and the line has been translated to mean: "He is beyond wearing out and being renewed", or: "He can renew himself before being worn out", or: "He can wear out without renewal", or even: "He can afford to seem worn out and not appear new." None of these translations give much meaning.

If we truly practice the Way we will not be filled up (4:1), but if we are not vigilant we may get caught up in the pride of attainments and desire for more. If we let such feelings fill us up, they will hinder further progress.

16:1

This describes a state of absorption in meditation called samadhi in Sanskrit.

16:2

In samadhi Lao Zi beholds the unity of life and death. Going back to the root is death. Death is quietness; it is also coming back to fate. Fate is the result of karma, which means action. The Tibetans say that in death an ordinary man is thrown into the stream of karmic results like a log pushed into a river, there is nothing more he can do. This is unfailing, therefore it is called constant. Only the one that has realized what is beyond life and death has overcome death. *Ming*, insight, is used in Buddhist scriptures meaning enlightenment.

16:3

The one who does not know that his fate is the result of his own actions will not be able to better his fate. The one who knows can step by step perfect himself until he has awakened the primal spirit to consciousness and thus is identified with that, which is beyond life and death.

17:1

So little is known of Lao Zi that his existence is doubted or flatly denied by most Western historians today.

17:2

If the leader has insufficient faith, the followers have no faith in him.

17:3

The way the sage works is so imperceptible that ordinary people believe they themselves naturally did it.

18:1

Goodwill and justice happen to be the virtues that Confucius encouraged. What Lao Zi is pointing out in this and the following chapter is that when the big words are being used it is a sign that the actual virtues are lacking.

18:2

This verse gives examples of the hypocrisy. The six relations are: Parent and child, elder and younger child, and husband and wife.

19:1

Embellishments is what Lao Zi calls the fair words, because he sees that the actions are soiled by selfishness and has nothing to do with true Virtue.

19:2

The last line is normally given as the first line of chapter 20, but it does rime with the two preceding lines and seem to belong here.

20:1

Agreement and flattery might seem to be the same, but if put to the test they differ, because there is no heart behind the flatterer's agreement and it can not be trusted.

Like and dislike seems very different, but in reality they are just random feelings, and sometimes the same object is liked at one time and disliked at another.

20:2

The meaning of these lines is uncertain. In some texts it could be translated; "What men fear they must fear", but I have chosen the meaning from the Ma Wang Dui text.

20:3

The Grand Sacrifice, *Tai Lao*, was the most elaborate feast, where three kinds of meat were offered.

That Lao Zi alone has cast anchor implies that the merry people are drifting without control.

20:4-6

In these verses Lao Zi shows the relative application of words by describing himself as seen by the worldlings: a mindless fool, a thickheaded brute. But ordinary people with their inquisitiveness and learning will get nowhere since the path cannot be entered by these means; to become one with the Way is not an intellectual matter (14:1, 48:1), it requires an empty mind (3:2, 11:2).

The Mother is synonymous with the Way (1:2), and to be fed by the Mother is to fill the belly with vital breath.

21:1

This chapter is essential to the understanding of the concept of Virtue as Lao Zi uses it.

When a man totally complies with the Way he gains Virtue, and this is how we must approach the Way, otherwise it is just disturbing and distracting.

21:2

What disturbs our peace of mind and distracts us from the essential is the images and the things (or substance), because they involve us in conflicting emotions of desire and repulsion. We must look for the essence, and when we experience its reality there is no room for doubt. In *The Secret of the Golden Flower* it is said: "These things are like when people drink water and know for themselves whether it is cool or warm: it is necessary for you to attain faith on your own."[*]

The three levels of the Way's manifestation: essence, image, and substance are implicit in chapters 1 and 10, as hinted at in the corresponding commentaries. Other religions have similar concepts. In Buddhism the Buddha's three bodies: Dharmakaya, the essence body; Sambhogakaya, the image body; and Nirmanakaya, the incarnation body. In Christianity the Trinity: The Holy Spirit is essence, the Father is image, and the Son is flesh.

21:3

The words "disturbing and distracting" calls to mind chapter 14, and there is a correspondence between the two chapters. In chapter 14, from the viewpoint of the beginner, the Way is baffling with its lack of form and substance; whereas here, after the affirmative experience of the essence, it is seen to contain all things.

"By this" means by having sorted the threads of the Way.

22:1

With the attainment of Virtue all faults are remedied, and by holding on to the Way, all needs are fulfilled (77:1-2, commentary 7:1).

22:3

"Perverted; then perfect" is a quotation from *The Classic on Rites.*

23:1

Compare with 5:3 and 56:1.

---

[*] The Secret of the Golden Flower translated by Thomas Cleary, Harper San Francisco, 1991, VI 11, p 36.

23:2-3

The principle that we unify ourselves with through our actions, whether it be the Way, Virtue, or failure, will prevail in our life. This is the law of karma or cause and effect (16:2-3).

24:1

"On tiptoe" means reaching too high; "astride" means spanning too wide. To be ambitious is to engage in failure.

24:2

These lines are the reverse of the lines in chapter 22 because engaging in failure is the opposite of embracing oneness.

25:1-3

Here Lao Zi comes back to the ultimate reality, how it was always there, how it must be the source of creation, and how, not knowing its true name, he has named it the Way. He calls it great and describes its cyclic movement.

25:4

The Chinese character for king is 王 *wang*. The three horizontal strokes represent earth, man, and heaven, while the vertical stroke that connects them represents the king as the enlightened intermediary between them; this is the reason that he is among the four greats.

25:5

The Way of heaven, the Way of earth, and the Way of man were early concepts in Chinese thought. Lao Zi is the first to use *Dao,* the Way, for the ultimate reality that was otherwise called *Tai Ji,* the Primal Beginning, and pictured like this ☯ .

26:1-3

Here yin - yang is symbolized by the pairs heavy - light and calm - quick-tempered.

As long as he lives, the sage holds on to the heavy or serene principle of the Receptive. The baggage-wagon is symbolic of the Receptive.* He is never moved to forget this by the glory of the world; if he as ruler lets go of the yin attitude and becomes frivolous and rash he will not endure.

27:1

The first line brings to mind the native Americans, who respect nature in much the same manner as the followers of the Way.

27:2

"Good shutting" refers to shutting out the sense impressions ("Shut the doors" in 52:2 and 56:2). "Good fastening" means fixing the mind in meditation. Fastening, *jie*, means both a knot and fix, firm, or constant — but the pun is lost in translation, or, if it is kept: "A good knot is done without tying a cord", the meaning becomes unclear.

---

* See *I Ching*, p. 275-6.

27:3-5

Helping others is to follow the insight. It is by helping others that the wonders of realization are approached, by those who have the skill. Those who have not, approach them by respecting and supporting their teachers.

28:1

The Virtue of a newborn infant is great because the subtle energies are still intact and in harmony (55:2).

28:3

The text has here been given various interpretations, as the third line can mean either that the sage uses the vessels (= able men), or that he is himself used, or that he uses the uncarved wood, i.e. practices simplicity. I have chosen this last meaning that seems to be confirmed by the last line. *Zhi*, carve, also means regulate or rule.

29:1-4

It is my belief that there has been a mix-up involving chapters 29, 42, and 64. These are the only places where there seem to be a break in the flow of the text, and since it can be remedied with a few transpositions I have taken the liberty to do so.

Here the third verse is taken from chapter 64 where it follows a verse identical to 29:2, and the last verse is taken from chapter 42.

31:2

"Noble man", *jun zi*, literally means child of a prince, but the esoteric meaning is the spiritual child of an enlightened being.

32:1-2

The Way's simple naturalness can never submit to the demands of the world, but it could conquer the world if induced by the example of the ruling classes. This would cause the union of heaven and earth, that is the hexagram *Tai*, Peace.

32:4

The Way comes alive in the world when a person is unified with it. Lao Zi again uses water as metaphor. Compared to the great Way such a person is only like a small rivulet - but it flows with the water of life.

Jesus said: "Whoever drinketh of the water that I shall give him shall never thirst; but the water that I shall give him shall be in him a well of water springing up into everlasting life." (John 4:14)

33:1

In *The Dhammapada* it is said: "Self-conquest is indeed far greater than the conquest of all other folk."[*]

33:2

In *The Dhammapada* it is said: "Contentment is the greatest wealth."[†]

"To act with strength" means to continually overcome oneself. "To die, yet not cease" is the same everlasting life that Jesus talks about.

34:1

The great river flooding and fertilizing the valley was the starting point for the early great civilizations. This is the image Lao Zi here calls up.

35:1-2

When the sage goes out in the world it is to transmit the great image, but he teaches by deeds, not by words (2:3), because words are dull and tasteless compared to music and sweetmeats.

35:3

These lines recall the beginning of chapter 14, and though the similarity is superficial, yet it points to meditation as the beginning of practice.

---

[*] *The Dhammapada* translated by Narada Thera, John Murray, London, 1954, VIII 104, p. 37.

[†] ibid, XV 204, p.57.

36:1

These principles are similar to those of the Japanese martial art Aikido: Join the movement of the adversary and add your force to his so that he overextends himself and fall. It is assuming the weak position in order to conquer (61:2).

36:2

The people cannot leave their level and should not be shown the tools of government (65:1).

Lao Zi does not advocate democracy; he does not think that the majority is in possession of wisdom, but rather that the clever ones among them will take action for their own advantage if they are not restrained (3:3). No system of government is better than the people who implement it. Lao Zi wants the unselfish in power, which is the logical solution - but it must be the true sage, for unselfishness is only incorruptible in the one who is unified with the Way.

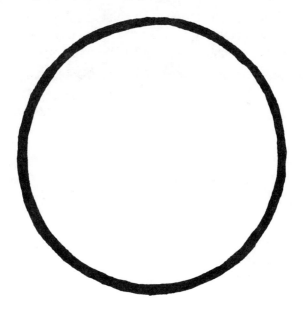

37:1-3

The Book of the Way is concluded with the path of no desire leading to a new Golden Age.

Somewhere in space-time a Golden Age exists. Since the movement of the Way is turning back (25:3), what is gone will come back, what is distant will come close.

It is evident that Lao Zi lived in times as troubled as ours; only in such times is it worth while to talk about the Way. If the Way is realized by all, what is there to say about it?

38:1

The Book of Virtue begins with a definition of Virtue compared to the inferior virtues of the world.

38:2

The inferior virtues are goodwill, justice, and propriety.

Goodwill has the superior quality of not acting for reasons, but out of compassion, while justice acts on cold reasoning and propriety is mere convention - and aggressive to boot.

Propriety, *li*, was always very strongly defined in Chinese society, a tendency that was upheld and strengthened by Confucianism (18:1-2, 19:1).

38:4

Here Lao Zi attacks living according to rules and preconceived ideas as the cause of worldly troubles and human folly. (See also commentary 48:1).

39:1

To attain oneness is to find equilibrium in interdependence — not a static equilibrium, but an equilibrium in cyclic movement. Individual separateness is an illusion; if we insist on it we are lost.

39:2

There is a warning to the ruler in this verse: If he lets go of oneness with the people, he will fall.

40:1

In Wang Bi this is chapter 41, but in Ma Wang Dui the order of the chapters 40 and 41 is reversed. I have followed Ma Wang Dui because it has a natural connection to chapter 42.

40:4

Square, *fang*, is derived from 卍 indicating the four corners of the world. Lao Zi states here that there are no corners, only figures of speech.

The great abilities are those of the sage.

The great tone is the AUM of creation — the music of the spheres — that is heard by few.

The great image is the Way .

41:1

"Turning back" refers to the practice of reversing the subtle energies as explained in the introduction under Daoist Yoga.

The common translation is also valid:

"Turning back is the movement of the Way;
"weakness is the function of the Way."

41:2

Physicist David Bohm says: "The physical matter has its root in the unmanifest."

42:1

The Way in its undifferentiated chaotic state is symbolized by $\bigcirc$.

It contains the potential for creation and is then called *Tai Ji* , the Great Primal Beginning, and is symbolized by ☯ .

It gives birth to the two primal principles yang and yin, the Creative and the Receptive.

When yang and yin is infused with the energy of the vital breath, *qi*, we have the yang spirit energy, *shen*, and the yin vital essence, *jing*, which is the sexual energy. From these three forms of energy all beings and all things are born.

42:2

The beings are different according to the balance of yang and yin.

42:3

It looks like those who abound in yin qualities are the losers, but the king knows that this is a superficial view and he identifies with the humble.

42:5

This verse is taken from chapter 29 (see commentary 29:1-4).

43:1

The softest thing in the world is water (78:1), which runs over the solid rock and wears it down.

Where there is a tiny crack only the most subtle can enter; where there is no crack at all only non-being, i.e. the Way, can enter. In the same way non-action can accomplish things that action would only spoil.

44:1-3

The importance of growing old is that it gives time to attain the great abilities (40:4). Therefore the body is most precious, as it is also taught in Buddhism.

45:1

To ordinary people things appear as the opposite of what they really are. The achievements of those who seek realization of the Way seem wanting, whereas the knowledge, opinions, and desires that fill up the worldly seem like vigor.

Here, as in chapter 4, most translators read *zhong*, an empty bowl, for *chong,* vigorous, and translate the third and fourth

lines: "Great fullness seems empty, in use it is not exhausted."
This seems to contradict what Lao Zi says about fullness f. ex. in
chapter 9: "To grasp at fullness is not like stopping." or in chapter 15: "Do not desire fullness."

Since it is necessary to amend the text in order to make sense, I
prefer to read *er*, and, for *bu*, not, in the last line.

45:3

In certain situations restlessness is appropriate, since in the
world of relativity everything has a positive aspect as well as a
negative. In relation to the practice, though, it is purity and
quietness that lead to the goal.

46:1

When the Way prevails the horses are only used in the fields
because the man of the Way has no reason to ride around (12:2,
47:2, 80:5).

46:2

To have many desires is to add to ones needs. In reality our
needs are simple and will readily be satisfied.

47:1-3

By staying in one place and living a simple life, the pattern of
things become apparent. When one can see the pattern, one can
see the big in the small and all things become clear.

48:1

We learn by endless accumulation of facts and methods until we
are filled up with knowledge. Such knowledge is frozen life, it is
like a block of ice that keeps the water of life from flowing. We
must melt this block, give up all beforehand knowledge, and let
life flow spontaneously (38:3).

48:2

To take power in the world with one's own fame and wealth as
motivation is bound to fail.

49:1

When the mind is not fixed in self-interest it can tune in to other minds and feel their feelings. This is true compassion.

49:2-3

Jesus said: "Bless them that curse you, do good to them that hate you." (Matt. 5:44)

I remember my teacher, Lama Yeshe, talking about pure love, and I asked him what he meant by that. "Pure love", he answered, "is love that is equal toward all sentient beings." His love was like that, pure, and through him the Way came alive in the world. Every day people came to him with their problems and their sorrows, and not one went away without having been comforted, like children comforted by their Mother.

50:1

"Three in ten" means roughly one third. There are people with three kinds of attitude. There are people that nurture life; caring, careful, and healthy; there are people that dare life; reckless, extremist, and in strife; and there are people that stupidly attach themselves to the flavors of life and thereby die spiritually. (The word *hou*, thick, also means flavorful or generous)

There is a parallel with the followers of the three gunas as described in *Bhagavad-Gita.** Sattva-people are the followers of life, rajas-people the followers of death, and tamas-people the ones that become like living dead by their concern for only material welfare.

Han Fei Zi (d. 233 B.C.) interprets *shi you san,* ten have three, as thirteen and the second to the fifth line goes:

"Life's followers are thirteen,
"death's followers are thirteen,
"men whose life move into dead ground,
"are also thirteen."

---

* See Bhagavad-Gita, p 107.

About half of the translators follow this interpretation .

50:2

To preserve life is the same as to gather Virtue, and the one who has great Virtue is protected by the Way (7:2, 55:1). His is not an unnatural death (29:4).

51:1

The Way is the cause of life.

Life is directed, sustained, and propagated by the subtle energies: spirit, vital breath, and vital essence. When the three energies are strong and harmonious there is Virtue, and life is nourished.

Thus Virtue starts the process of growth, but substance decides the shape by means of the genes, and as we grow into the world the influence of our environment decides the final outcome.

51:2

That all beings venerate the Way and value Virtue is obvious since all cling to life and pursue nourishment; that comes natural.

51:3

Life comes from the Way, but its progress in the world depends on the strength and harmony of the subtle energies; the more Virtue the better quality of life.

51:4

For the energies within to be in harmony there must be harmony also without. This unselfish attitude is an expression of the perfection of Virtue.

52:1

This chapter is about the method of turning back from the world and holding on to the Way. When the union with the Way is achieved one has overcome death (16:2-3).

52:2

By stopping the outflow of sexual energy through the sex organ and the outflow of spirit energy through the sense organs the body will keep its vitality. By letting the energies flow out the body will be depleted of its vitality.

Pleasure-gate, 兑 *dui*, means both mouth or opening and joy or pleasure. It is the name of the trigram ☱ Lake.

52:3

To see the small is to be very perceptive in one's practice. To keep to the yielding is to practice without exertion (6:2) and to live in the world without strife (8:3).

52:4

This verse refers to "turning the light around" as described in *The Secret of the Golden Flower*. According to master Lu Zi, who lived at the end of the eighth and the beginning of the ninth century, the expression "turning the light around" was revealed by Wenshi, a disciple of Lao Zi. The Light is the conscious spirit; when turned around it brings the primal spirit into consciousness. That is enlightenment or the original insight restored (6:1).

53:1-3

In this chapter Lao Zi talks about those of the ruling class who does not "turn back and keep to the Mother." The implication of the second verse is that the peasants are conscripted to clean the courts and therefore have no time for their fields.

54:1-3

The way to firmly establish Virtue in the world begins in one-self. H. H. the 14th Dalai Lama used almost identical words to point out how peace in the world must grow out of peace in the individual mind.

55:1

When Virtue is firmly established we are like newborn into

another level of energy, protected from the stings of the world (7:2, 50:2).

55:2

In the newborn the subtle energies are strong and harmonious; that is the reason Lao Zi compares one who has great Virtue with a newborn infant (20:3, 28:1).

The inner Virtue is described as vitality, the outer as harmony.

55:3

"Knowing the constant is called insight". This was also said in chapter 16 in the context of overcoming death. Here it is connected with the method: increasing life by not letting the subtle energies flow out, but turning them back by the help of breath meditation.

In *The Secret of the Golden Flower* it is said that "when mind is subtle, breath is subtle; when mind is unified it moves energy."* Therefore, applying the mind to the vital breath is a starting point in the yoga of reviving the primal spirit.

A majority of translators misunderstand the last two lines taking *xiang* to mean 'ill omen'. This is against inner evidence in the text: in chapter 31 *xiang* obviously means 'auspicious' in "weapons are not auspicious tools", and the same is the case in 78:3 (where 'not auspicious' is given as 'misfortunes'). It is also unreasonable to give a negative connotation to the expression "...is called strength" that Lao Zi employs in a positive sense in chapter 52: "To keep to the yielding is called strength."

The reason for twisting the meaning here is, I think, a scholarly bias against Eastern mysticism — unfortunate in translators of a text of Eastern mysticism.

55:6

If we let the energies flow out in the ordinary way by procre-

---

* *The Secret of the Golden Flower*, IV 10, p.25.

ation and attachment to worldly pleasures we will become old and decrepit and, as the Buddhists say, 'die in vain.'

56:1

To talk of one's experiences and attainments in this practice is a serious loss of energy. It is a common experience how great determination can evaporate in talk, and all yogic traditions agree in recommending silence about one's achievements.

56:2

The first two lines are already explained in commentary 52:2.

The next four lines are repeated from 4:2, and my interpretation is as follows:

"The sharp" refers to the emotions; "the tangled" to the attachments. "Harmonizing the light" refers to the work of transferring the one bright line from the trigram *Kan*, Water, to the trigram *Li*, Fire (commentary 6:1, 52:4). To "unify the dispersed" refers to the unification of the Creative, Heaven, and the Receptive, Earth. This is the primordial union that is the "door of all wonders" (1:4, commentary 6:1). It is pictured in the hexagram *Tai*, Peace (commentary 10:1-2, 32:2).

56:3

When the supreme union is achieved one is beyond the entanglements of the world; then one has perfect equanimity (49:2) and unshakeable equilibrium (13:1-3).

In *The Dhammapada* it is said: "Whoso is perfect in virtue and insight ... him do folk hold dear."*

57:1-3

This chapter describes the straight means to govern in accord with the Way.

---

* *The Dhammapada*, XVI 217, p. 59.

In waging war, which is essentially against the cultivation of the Way, the extraordinary becomes the means of upholding the Way. This is described in chapters 68 and 69: retreating instead of advancing, and not engaging with the enemy.

58:1

In chapter 20 Lao zi said: "Worldly men are inquisitive and meddlesome, I alone am hesitant and reserved." Here he contrasts his kind of government with current government (both at his time and at ours).

58:2

In the world today the gap between rich and poor is widening and there is no doubt that the luck of those of us who live in a wealthy sector are leaning on the misfortune of those who are not; as their misfortune is prostrating to our luck. The exploitation has become global, and we must certainly ask with Lao Zi: "Who knows how far it will go?" We seem to be a lot closer to the limit than was Lao Zi. When he got enough he took his buffalo, passed over the mountains, and disappeared. If I would try that I would arrive in Silicon Valley.

In the second line the character 伏 *fu*, lay prostrate, consists of 人 man and 犬 dog i.e. a man who is like a dog or lives a dog's life. I take it to mean that misfortune is subjected to luck, and not, as most translators believe, that misfortune is lurking in luck.

59;1

As the enlightened intermediary between ordinary people and heaven, the king's duty is to rule men and serve heaven (see commentary 25:4). In order to be fit for this he must conserve his subtle energies from he is very young and submit to the practice of fusing them in harmony, so he can gather a heavy store of Virtue.

H. H. the Dalai Lama started his education when he was four years old.

59:3

With a heavy store of Virtue the king can get the country, but only if he reaches the supreme union with the Mother will he become like the kings of the Golden Age.

60:1

Small fish must be cooked without stirring, or they will fall apart.

60:2-3

Demons have no power over the man of the Way. It is told that when the great Indian magician, Padma Sambhava, came to Tibet to spread the Buddhist teachings, his work was obstructed by demons, but his magic was stronger than theirs, and they were subdued and became powerful protectors of the Dharma (teachings). Thus they became virtuous and their power added to that of Padma Sambhava, and Buddhism began to flourish in Tibet.

61:1

The word *jiao*, confluence, has several meanings: associate with, have intercourse with, etc. It was tempting to use the translation melting-pot in order to associate the great country with the United States, except it violates the water metaphor.

Lao Zi uses female-male polarity synonymous with yin-yang. That was natural in his time and culture, and biologically it will always be true, but mentally there is of course no reason that it could not be the opposite.

61:2-3

Nowadays the great countries seem to be the bullies of the world, and they do not conquer the small countries as f.ex. Vietnam and Afghanistan. If there is any solution to the contemporary problems in the world, they lie along the line of Lao Zi's teaching.

62:1

The character *ao*, hidden, pictures the dark corners of the house, where the treasures are stored and where one cannot see, but only discern by groping with the hands. It is also the place where the house gods are worshipped.

This is how the Way is hidden in the beings.

62:2

In chapter 81 Lao Zi says: "Fair words are not truthful." Thus fair words are only for the marketplace, but a noble example can elevate a man, and if a man can be helped he should not be rejected. This is an unusual interpretation of the first line, but logical considering Lao Zi's aversion to words (5:3, 23:1, 35:2, 43:2).

62:3

The enthronement of an emperor is not an everyday event. A king or a prince might think it important to be present on such an occasion, but, says Lao Zi, to meditate is more important.

The jade disc was held in front of the mouth with both hands, so that one's breath would not encroach on the Son of Heaven.

62:4

"Ask, and it shall be given you," says Jesus (Matt. 7:7).

One might think that Jesus knew Lao Zi's teachings since so many of his important sayings are identical, but of course a simple explanation is that as enlightened beings, they knew the same truth.

63:1-2

"The tasteless" is another name for the Way.

To repay injury with Virtue means to repay with goodness and faith (49:2).

65:2

Cleverness is Lao Zi's term for the intelligence that uses its knowledge of others to manipulate them in its own interest (3:3). When the country is governed by people with this quality, it is being ruined.

65:3

Know the difference between cleverness and insight (33:1). The pattern to follow is to reject cleverness and turn back to the simple virtues described in chapter 19: "Look plain and cherish simplicity, be without selfishness and have fewer desires, abolish learning and have no worries."

65:4

Supreme Virtue is truly powerful as it is described in chapter 37

The character 順 *shun*, compliance, consists of 川 stream and 頁 head; when all heads follow the great stream — an image of the Way — there is no difficulty in ruling and the country is blessed.

67:1

The Way is absolute, everything else is relative; therefore the Way is great and will ever stay great. If any relative thing was set up as great, its lack of true greatness would be apparent when it was compared to something even greater.

67:2-3

Here Lao Zi indicates the qualities that make a true hero. The three primary qualities are compassion, frugality, and humbleness; the three derived from them are courage, generosity, and the highest abilities to lead.

67:4

Without the inner yin qualities the derived yang qualities cannot be sustained.

67:5

The treasure above all treasures is compassion.

H. H. the Dalai Lama of Tibet is the bodhisattva of compassion incarnate. As a ruler he is a vestige of the Golden Age, and our depraved times has robbed him of his executive power, but as he has lost his country, his influence has spread all over the world with his message of compassion as the prerequisite of peace.

68:1-2, 69:1-2

War is not in accord with the Way, but it is an issue one cannot pass by. In chapters 30 and 31 Lao Zi has explained how weapons are not of the Way. In these chapters he talks about victory in fight and firmness in defence (67:5).

If one is attacked one must in some way respond, if one's home is threatened one must defend it. Lao Zi's straightforward means of upholding the Way under such circumstances, namely to retreat and not engage with the enemy, will by most be seen as "abnormal" (57:1, 58:3), but to respond with anger and aggression is to be contaminated by what you fight.

"Whomsoever shall compel thee to go a mile, go with him twain," says Jesus (Matt. 5:41). Lao Zi is just as pacific, but more like: 'If one will force you to go a mile, let him run after you till he gets tired.' That is Chinese practicality.

69:3

Anger, greed, and pride are the inner enemies; if they are taken lightly one might lose the three treasures: compassion, frugality, and humbleness.

Note how Lao Zi often when he seems to be talking about the outer world is actually referring to the inner world.

70:1

Lao Zi's words are easy to understand for the one who can give up knowledge accumulated through learning; they are easy to act upon for the one who can give up all selfish concern. Since our personality and our learning reinforce each other and seem to be our very identity, few can give them up; worldly people certainly can not.

70:2

The ancestors of Lao Zi's words are his experiences of the wonderful essence of the Way (21:2); his actions are governed by his Virtue (49:2). Because essence and Virtue are not known by the worldly, they do not understand Lao Zi.

70:3

In China wool was the simple man's clothing, while silk was for the upper class.

71:1

To know what is not known by the multitude of people is superior. To be ignorant of that which is known by the sages is to be sick. In Buddhism ignorance is the root cause of being bound to the wheel of life, i.e. the cycle of birth and death and the different realms of suffering. To be sick of this unending round of misery is the only thing that can prod us into looking for enlightenment.

The text here is very terse and has received many explanations. Most have some truth, but since Lao Zi has just been talking about what is not known — the ancestors of his words and the ruler of his deeds — it seems reasonable to assume that he is referring to this.

72:1

Since the king is united with the Way (16:3, commentary 25:4), to fear his might is equivalent to godfearing in Christian terminology.

When the people are no more godfearing, then the mighty visitations will come: the wars and poverty of a world where hatred and greed are unleashed.

72:2

To make the people fear his might the king should not pry into their lives or make them weary of their work; this kind of abuse is exactly what in the end calls forth rebellion.

73:1

This is to say that there is no absolute right action; sometimes killing may be necessary and right. No one can untangle the threads of fate (karma), even the sage considers it difficult.

73:2

The Way of heaven is yielding, yet it is effective.

73:3

Whatever action we chose to take it will not slip unnoticed through heavens net; it will have its consequences. Knowledge of right action depends on a pure heart, but if we follow the Way of heaven we never go wrong (77:1).

74:1-2

The fear of death is a way to keep people in awe of the ruler. As Lao Zi says in the preceding chapter, killing can sometimes benefit, but it is difficult to know when; therefore the ruler should be wary of using his power to kill, because it could easily harm himself.

75:1

He Shang Gong entitled this chapter "Greed harms." Lao Zi places the responsibility for starvation and social unrest with the government. The greed of the ruling class contaminates the people, who think only of obtaining the gifts of life and do not think of death. We should take death seriously, because in death we cannot better our fate (16:3).

75:2

People are unwise in valuing life's abundance and striving to have part in it; it only leads them into dead ground (50:1).

78:3

Each state had its fertility shrine and the autonomy of the state depended on the ruler's ability to be master of the shrine.

That the ruler should accept the disgrace and bad omens of the country was a common idea in Chinese antiquity as well as in other cultures and is similar to Christ taking upon himself the sins of all mankind.

79:2

Contracts were written on two slips of bamboo, notched so that they fit together. There is a certain lack of clarity here; not only are there texts that have 'right' instead of 'left' (f.ex. the oldest Ma Wang Dui), but also the experts disagree as to which side was held by the creditor, which by the debtor. Most texts have 'left' and I believe that the left side was held by the debtor, otherwise the text makes no sense.

79:3

The Way is impartial, but since the good man follows the Way he will be with it, and it will be with him.

Shri Krishna said: "My face is equal to all creation, loving no one nor hating any. Nevertheless, my devotees dwell within me always: I also show forth and am seen within them."*

80:3

Prior to writing, knotted cords were the means of keeping record.

In Lao Zi's vision of a Golden Age there is great contentment; we are far from the modern world of fast food, polyester clothes, TV's blaring stupidity and violence, and the uninhibited commercialism of any special events.

80:4

Lao Zi envisions complete decentralization, his country is more like a village.

81:3

The book is not composed as linear argumentation starting at zero and ending with the conclusion; it is rather like Indra's net of pearls where each pearl reflects the totality of creation.

---

* *Bhagavad-Gita*, p. 84.

TEXTUAL NOTES

The textual notes indicate any departure from the standard text by Wang Bi.

2:3

The following has been moved to chapter 51: "This is how the myriad beings arise and do not refuse..." and two lines that are already in chapter 51 has been omitted:

"To give life, but not possess;
"to act, but not rely upon it."

4:1

For *huo*, maybe, read: *you*, be (Ma Wang Dui).

5:3

For *shu*, reckon, read: *shu*, quickly (Ma Xu Lun).

9:1

For *zhuo*, stick, read: *rui*, keen.

10:2

For *wu*, without, read: *wei*, do (Fu Yi).

15:1

For *shi*, scholar, read: *dao*, way (Fu Yi).

15:2

For *yan*, how, read: *xi,* oh.

For *rong*, appearance, read: *ke*, guest (He Shang Gong).

After the fifth line insert two lines from chapter 20 whose construction and meaning suggest that they belong here:

"Placid, they were like the sea;
"steady, as a wind that never stops."

17:3

For *you,* distant, read: *you,* deliberate (Ma Wang Dui).

20:5

Omit:

"Placid, they were like the sea;
"steady, as a wind that never stops." that has been moved to 15:2.

21:3

For: "From ancient times up till now," read: "From the present back to ancient times." (Ma Wang Dui).

23:2

Omit *dao zhe,* way they.

A few texts repeat *cong shi yu,* engaging in, in the third and fifth lines, which then become similar in construction to the first line. I have adopted this interpretation.

28:2

Omit:

"Adhering to his black,
"he is a model under heaven.
"Being a model under heaven,
"his constant Virtue is not erring;
"he returns to the infinite.
"Knowing his glory."

The verses are quoted by Zhuang Zi (Chuang Tzu) without these lines, and they do not add anything to what is said.

30:3

In the sixth line add *ju,* dwell upon, and in the seventh line add *shi wei,* this is called.

Omit the lines that recur in chapter 55:

"When beings are healthy,

"and then become decrepit,
"it is called not the Way.
"What is not the Way soon ends."(Yao Nai).

29:3

This verse is taken from chapter 64 (See commentary 29:1-4).

29:4

This verse is taken from chapter 42 (See commentary 29:1-4).

31:1

Omit *zui*, fine (Ma Wang Dui).

35:2

For *kou*, mouth, read: *yan*, word (Ma Wang Dui).

37:1

For *you*, have, read: *wei,* do (He Shang Gong).

38:2

After the second line omit:

"Inferior Virtue is doing,
"and is doing for a reason." (Ma Wang Dui).

39:4

For *yu*, carriage, read: *yu,* honor (Wu Cheng).

For *lao*, necklace, read: *lao,* leave alone (He Shang Gong).

40:5

For *dai,* lend, read: *shi*, begin (Ma Wang Dui).

Insert *shan*, good, in the last line (Ma Wang Dui).

42:3

For *xu*, sob, read: *je*, warmhearted (Ma Wang Dui).

For *zuo*, subdue, read: *zai,* sustain (He Shang Gong).

This verse is taken from chapter 29 (See commentary 29:1-4).

45:1

For *bu*, not, read: *er*, and, in the last line (See commentary 45:1)

46:2

Add the first line:

"There is no greater crime than many desires." (He Shang Gong).

49:3

For *xi*, inhale, read: *xi*, amiable, compliant.

After the third line insert:

"Ordinary-people lend him their ears and eyes." (Fu Yi & He Shang Gong)

51:3

Add the line: "This is how the myriad beings arise and do not refuse…" from chapter 2 and "Life and nourishment" from 10:3 (= "Give life and nourish.").

55:2

For *quan,* perfect, read: *zun,* penis (Ma Wang Dui).

60:3

Omit *ren,* man, in the second line (Ma Wang Dui).

62:3

For *gong*, impartial, read: *ching*, minister (Ma Wang Dui).

64:1

For *pan*, college, read: *po*, break (Carus).

64:3

The following lines have been omitted here and moved to chapter 29 where the first four of them were already extant:

"If you interfere with it,
"you will ruin it.

"If you grasp it,
"you will lose it.

"Therefore the sage does not interfere;
"thus he ruins nothing.
"He does not grasp;
"thus he loses nothing." (See commentary 29:1-4).

65:3

For *ji*, check, read: *kai*, pattern (He Shang Gong).

76:1

In the third line omit *wan wu,* myriad beings.

76:2

For *bing*, weapon, read: *zhe*, break (Fu Yi).